# GODS MERCIE

## MIXED WITH HIS JUSTICE

OR

HIS PEOPLES DELIVERANCE IN TIMES OF DANGER
(1641)

BY

## JOHN COTTON

A FACSIMILE REPRODUCTION

WITH AN INTRODUCTION

BY

## EVERETT H. EMERSON

*Lehigh University*

GAINESVILLE, FLORIDA

SCHOLARS' FACSIMILES & REPRINTS

1958

SCHOLARS' FACSIMILES & REPRINTS
118 N.W. 26TH STREET
GAINESVILLE, FLORIDA
HARRY R. WARFEL, GENERAL EDITOR

REPRODUCED FROM TWO COPIES IN

AND WITH THE PERMISSION OF

YALE UNIVERSITY LIBRARY

L. C. CATALOG CARD NUMBER: 58-5651

MANUFACTURED IN THE U.S.A.
LETTERPRESS BY WAYSIDE PRESS
PHOTOLITHOGRAPHY BY EDWARDS BROTHERS
BINDING BY UNIVERSAL DIXIE BINDERY

# INTRODUCTION

Of the first three great New England preachers, Thomas Hooker, Thomas Shepard, and John Cotton, Cotton has been regarded as definitely the least interesting and effective, so far as scholars have been able to judge from his published writings which have come down to us. Nearly every student of Puritanism in the last hundred years who has discussed Cotton's writings has expressed disappointment with what he has found. Moses Coit Tyler may be regarded as typical. "Let us open now," suggests Tyler, "any of these old books of John Cotton. At once, the immensity of his contemporaneous influence becomes a riddle to us. . . . Evidently the vast intellectual and moral force of John Cotton was a thing that could not be handed over to the printing-press or transmitted to posterity: it had to communicate itself in the living presence of the man himself."

The reason for modern disappointment with Cotton may perhaps be explained without difficulty. Of Cotton's thirty-four published works, sixteen are concerned with matters of church polity and discipline; such titles as *Singing of Psalmes a Gospel-Ordinance* and *A modest and Cleare Answer to Mr. Ball's Discourse of set formes of Prayer* are hardly likely to be of much interest today. Of the remainder, the largest number, twelve, are sermons; for one reason or another several of these disqualify themselves for our interest by nature of their subject matter. Three are expositions of the Book of Revelation, a happy hunting ground for those who sought Biblical comment on current affairs. (Cotton was such a seeker.) Another long work reveals by its title the reason for its lack of modern appeal: *A Briefe Exposition of the Whole Book of Canticles, or Song of Solomon: Lively describing the Estate of the Church in all the ages thereof, both Jewish and Christian, to this day. And modestly pointing at the Gloriousnesse of the restored Estate of the Church of the Jewes, and the happy accesse of the Gentiles, in the approaching days of Reformation, when the Wall of Petition shall be taken away.* (This work was reprinted in Edinburgh in 1866.)

If Cotton's reputation as a writer were to be salvaged, it could rest rather securely on such volumes as *The Way of Life* (1641), *A Sermon . . . Delivered at Salem* (not published till 1713), and the six sermons in the present volume. *Gods Mercie mixed with his Justice* has a virtue which neither the much longer *The Way of Life* (481 pages) nor the single sermon has: it is concentrated but long enough to provide the modern reader with an adequate sample of the range of Cotton's mind, his method of handling religious doctrine, and his strengths and weaknesses as a preacher.

I

The typical product of the Puritan mind is not philosophical theology such as we find in the works of the Anglican Richard Hooker or the Catholic Thomas Aquinas. Puritan theological treatises are few in number, limited in scope, and derivative in matter. Nor is it the devotional tract or the disputation, though many flowed from Puritan pens. The essential Puritan is revealed in the sermon, and the heart of the Puritan sermon is the application of doctrine, not the doctrine itself.

Nevertheless it is helpful to understand clearly the fundamental beliefs of such a Puritan as Cotton. The essence of Cotton's theology, one can assume, is contained in his famous catechism, *Milk for Babes*. Though less well known, Cotton's "Twelve Fundamental Articles of the Christian Religion" is perhaps more reliable since it is addressed to adults, not children. It was published in 1713 as part of *A Treatise 1. Of Faith*. Here Cotton affirms belief in the Trinity; maintains that God made and governs the world, rewards the good and punishes the evil; teaches that God is to be worshipped according to His written Word. Man, he believes, has been completely sinful since the Fall and can do nothing to save himself. Therefore the Son of God became man and redeemed His Church. Salvation comes by faith, which is given by God through the Word and the Spirit. The process consists of justification by faith and regeneration, which remains imperfect in this world. The regenerate are saved at Judgment Day, when the wicked are damned.

This statement of belief helps explain the Puritan concern for the sermon. The faith which saves comes through the Word (that is, the Gospel), and, as Cotton explains elsewhere, normally faith comes from hearing the Word preached, not by reading either the Bible or sermons. Yet Puritanism insisted that it was not the preached Word *per se* which brought saving grace; such a view would make the preacher responsible for salvation. Rather the preached Word accompanies God's Spirit, as an outward sign of the inner force. Thus Cotton insists that his hearers come to church with no trust in the sermon itself: "... trust not in the meanes; pray to Christ, to blesse the Ordinances to you; and intreat him to cleanse your hearts and hands from those evils that are in his sight, and come trusting on him, not in any strength in the meanes, and then he will be found of you, if you seeke him in truth" (*Christ the Fountain of Life*, 1657, pp. 24-25).

On the other hand, the Puritan preacher had to prepare his sermons as if he himself were responsible for the salvation of his hearers' souls. Cotton indirectly described the preparation of a sermon in the preface to a collection of sermons by his fellow Puritan Arthur Hildersam: "When Schollers furnish themselues with store of other writers, besides the Scriptures, and being little conversant in the Scriptures, to draw the Scriptures to the Authors, whom they most affect, and not their Authors to the Scriptures, their Diuinity prooueth but Humanity, and their Ministry speaketh to the braine, but not to the conscience of the Hearer. But he that diggeth all the Treasures of his knowledge, and the ground of Religion out of the Scriptures, and maketh use of other Authors, not for ostentation of himselfe, nor for the ground of his faith, nor for the principall ornament of his Ministry, but for the better searching out of the deepe wisdome of the Scriptures, such an one belieueth what he teacheth, not by an humane Credulity from his Author, but by a diuine faith from the Word: and because he belieueth, he therefore speaketh: and speaking from faith in his owne heart, he speaketh much more powerfully unto the begetting and strengthening of faith in the Hearer" (*Lectures Upon . . . John*, 1629, A3v).

As might be expected, Cotton does not always cite the authors whom he found useful in preparing his works. Those whom he does cite can perhaps be taken as representative of the kind of reading which he did in preparation. John Calvin's writings are referred to most frequently, as might be expected from Cotton's famous declaration that he sweetened his mouth nightly with Calvin's works. Next follow, in order of frequency of reference, Cardinal Bellarmine, the great controversialist whom Cotton felt continually obliged to refute; St. Augustine; Junius, the popular Reformed theologian; Theodore Beza, Calvin's successor; Aristotle; and William Ames, probably the greatest theologian of Puritanism. Many others are cited, some of whom one may be surprised to find: Horace, Avicenna, and Boethius.

It is well known that before his conversion to Puritanism Cotton was famous as a learned preacher and that afterwards he became a plain preacher following the model of William Perkins. Obviously Cotton did not forget his learning nor his wit overnight. In the sermons which were later published as *A Practicall Commentary . . . Upon The First Epistle Generall of John* (1658), Cotton supplies his reader with the reasons which the Schoolmen render for Christ's not becoming an angel and a discussion of why the oracles stopped at the time of the Nativity. In the present volume there are other examples of Cotton's scholarliness, as we shall see. Mr. Zoltan Haraszti does well to call Cotton "a Puritan scholastic steeped in medieval habits of thought."

## II

*Gods Mercie mixed with his Justice* is not well named (presumably it was not Cotton's title), for only the third sermon is on the subject of these attributes of God, and they are dealt with there in a rather special context. But each sermon is significant because each reveals an important aspect of Puritanism. The first sermon is on a text frequently chosen by Puritan preachers. (Compare Thomas Hooker's discussion of the text in *The Unbeleevers Preparing for Christ*, 1638, Pt. I, pp. 25-26.) It seems to have been used, first, because it dramatizes the position of the preacher, who stands as God's spokesman, knocking on men's hearts with his sermons. Secondly, the metaphorical language of the text permitted Cotton, the plain preacher, an excuse to be witty enough to deliver a lively sermon. We shall note that three other sermons in the book likewise employ a good deal of metaphorical language. Thirdly, the text permits, indeed invites, a voluntaristic approach to the conversion process, and even thorough-going Calvinists were aware of the difficulty of preaching predestination for the purpose of conversion, Cotton's purpose here.

The picture of God as waiter, taking orders from the redeemed, serving up a proper morsel to his children, strikes one as lacking appropriate dignity, though the same kind of homely imagery is fundamental in the poetry of a later Puritan pastor, Edward Taylor. The central image in the sermon is more effective: God beating on the door of man's heart. The image is sustained and developed at some length. Cotton explains why God knocks and how He knocks, and then how man may open the door to God by faith, confession, and willingness to submit to God's will. He ends the sermon by explaining the glories that come from opening the door. The only suggestion that God is master and controls the redemptive process is a brief paragraph (pages 12-13) in which Cotton says that God "many times" after much knocking opens the door Himself. But even this paragraph is far from teaching that God's grace is irresistible, the orthodox Reformed position.

The second sermon is not dominated by a single image, though the concept of being washed white by the mire of tribulation is the subject of several pages; it is designed apparently to enliven the sermon and seems partly successful, though the conceit describing the discovery of Christ's blood in a mixture of mire and water may strike the reader as both disgusting and too artificial.

The second sermon is an interesting example of a technique used repeatedly by preachers of Cotton's time, for instance, by both Thomas Hooker and Thomas Shepard in their series of sermons on the redemptive process. On the one hand Cotton's sermon is a detailed description, a piece of expository prose, explaining that God's redeemed must expect to experience many troubles, which however are not beyond what they can bear, and that these trials serve to improve greatly the religious principles and practice of those so tried. On the other hand, the sermon is advice and encouragement to its hearers; their afflictions can be used to help them improve themselves. The fact that a sermon was also a treatise, was indeed often labeled a treatise in its published form, resulted perhaps from the Puritan habit of note-taking. The passion and personal appeal of a sermon cannot be easily captured in notes, but if a sermon is a systematic treatise, the notes may be of considerable value.

The third sermon is an unusual one, for whereas most Puritan sermons are addressed to the unconverted, the converted, or both, this sermon is addressed to the unconverted who are members of the Church—members, that it, of a "particular visible church." Such a church, formed by covenant, Cotton had helped establish in Boston in Lincolnshire before coming to America. One of the fundamental problems of this convenanting, congregational Puritanism was to determine who are the truly converted, for to qualify for membership in such a church, one had to convince the other members that he had indeed been converted, though fallible man could never be absolutely certain of the state of his fellows. Let Cotton speak of it: each would-be member "maketh confession of his sinnes, and profession of his faith. In confession of his sinnes (that it may appeare to be a penitent confession) he declareth also the grace of God to his soule, drawing him out of his sinfull estate into fellowship with Christ. . . . though wee willingly admit all commers to the hearing of the Word with us . . . yet we receive none as members into the Church but such as (according to the judgement of charitable Christians) may be conceived to be received of God into fellowship with Christ, the head of the Church. . . . Nevertheless, in this triall, wee doe not exact eminent measure, either of knowledge, or holinesse, but doe willingly stretch out our hands to receive the weake in faith, such in whose spirits wee can discerne the least measure of breathing and panting after Christ, in their sensible feeling of a lost estate; for we had rather 99. hypocrites should perish through presumption, then one humble soule belonging to Christ, should sinke under discouragement or despaire; and by reason of the hypocrites received into the church, it is that the Church is said to have good and bad, wheate and tares; for tares, (as Hierome saith) are like to wheate" (*The Way of the Churches of Christ in New England,* 1645, pages 55-58).

One notes that Cotton refers to hypocrites as evil members. They are evil, of course, because they are still in the natural state of total depravity. The many aspects of resemblance between evil members and the briars and thorns of Cotton's text provide occasion for a good deal of wit which brightens up the sermon.

The fourth, fifth, and sixth sermons are almost one continuous piece. Presumably repetitious material at the beginning of the last two sermons was omitted for the sake of readability, although the first of the three also seems abbreviated. The first two are less interesting because Cotton found little opportunity to exercise his wit. However, the first is a useful sample of Cotton's ability as an exegete; he was proud of the fact that there were no difficult passages in all of the Bible which he had not explained to his own satisfaction. Further, the sermon demonstrates the Puritan delight in reading an anti-Roman Catholic prophecy from the Book of Revelation.

In the fifth sermon Cotton's love of method prevented his making his material interesting to modern readers. We stumble over the "secondly's" and "thirdly's." Cotton's desire to explain exhaustively the ways in which man can tempt God to act seems far removed from the expected Puritan piety and morality. Still, method was an important aspect of the Puritan sermon.

The final sermon is one of the most interesting, partly because of what it shows about Cotton's interest in science. As Professor Theodore Hornberger has pointed out, pages 113-114, in which Cotton discusses natural causes, are well-grounded in the older science. This interest of Cotton in science is another indication of his learning and should be considered in the light of his remark elsewhere that "To study the nature and course, and use of all Gods works, is a duty imposed by God upon all sorts of men; from the King that sitteth upon the Throne to the Artificer" (*A Briefe Exposition . . . upon . . . Ecclesiastes,* 1654, page 23).

Although one cannot generalize and say that Cotton's view of science is typically Puritan, another aspect of the sermon perhaps can be so labeled. Cotton implies throughout this sermon that belief in Christ is rational and is comparable to belief in the truths of science. Such an idea is of course foreign to Calvinism and foreign to Cotton's own position as stated elsewhere. "By nature we are blinde," Cotton teaches in *The Way of Life,* "and have not an eye open to looke at Christ, much lesse fasten upon him. It is grace alone by which wee see sinnes against Christ" (page 20). Cotton's inconsistency is typical of the Puritanism of his time, which was still paying lip-service to the strict Calvinism of the Synod of Dort, while at the same time finding that the times demanded a more liberal, more voluntaristic viewpoint. But Cotton makes much less use of the doctrine of predestination than do some of his contemporaries, such as Thomas Hooker. When Cotton refers to the doctrine, it is likely to be in reproving those who excuse their sins on the grounds of predestination.

This sermon is probably as attractive from a literary point of view as anything Cotton wrote. The mixture of wit and learning makes the sermon far better than most seventeenth-century Puritan sermons in the plain style, better than the sermons of such Puritan notables as Richard Sibbes and John Preston.

What may surprise readers of Cotton's sermons is the very little that is said about the practical problems of everyday living, problems which the converted if not the uncalled should be concerned with. Although one imagines that Cotton advocated a high ethical standard (we know that he preached a sermon in Massachusetts on the just price), little is said about these matters in any of his published sermons. Highly detailed and practical treatises on ethical matters were written by many Puritans, among them William Perkins and Richard Baxter. Why we have no really practical works by John Cotton is difficult to explain.

## III

Matthias Swallowe, author of the epistle "To the Christian Reader" of *Gods Mercie mixed with his Justice,* was graduated from Queen's College, Cambridge, in 1623. At the time he wrote the epistle he was minister at St. Bride's, London. None of his own works seems to have been published. In a style which is an interesting contrast to Cotton's, he explains as much as we know about the sermons which make up *Gods Mercie.* They were delivered in England, which Cotton left for America in 1633, when he was forty-eight.

*Gods Mercie* was reissued with a new title page in 1658 and entitled *The Saints Support & Comfort, in The Time of Distress and Danger, with Divers other Treatises, Delivered in severall sermons upon Divers Texts of Scripture.*

I wish to thank the Lehigh University Institute of Research, the Folger Shakespeare Library, and Miss Marjorie G. Wynne of the Yale University Library for their assistance.

*Lehigh University*                            EVERETT H. EMERSON

# BIBLIOGRAPHICAL NOTE

The first published life of John Cotton was John Norton's *Abel being Dead yet speaketh* (1658). Cotton's grandson Cotton Mather included a longer life in his *Magnalia Christi Americana* (1702). Two important recent dissertations on Cotton provide the fullest accounts, though they remain unpublished. Donald R. Come, "John Cotton, Guide of the Chosen People" (Princeton, 1949), provides much background information, especially for Cotton's American years. Judith B. Welles, "John Cotton, 1584-1652, Churchman and Theologian" (Edinburgh, 1948), is especially useful for Cotton's English background. An excellent short account appears in Williston Walker's *Ten New England Leaders* (New York, 1901). Cotton's sermon on the just price is discussed in John Winthrop's *Journal*. Theodore Hornberger has treated Cotton's attitude toward science in the *New England Quarterly*, X (1937), 503-515. Perry Miller's *Orthodoxy in Massachusetts* (Cambridge, Mass., 1933) provides a detailed study of Cotton's Congregationalism. A good special study is the unpublished master's essay by Wayne H. Christy, "John Cotton: Covenant Theologian" (Duke, 1942). Zoltan Haraszti has some interesting remarks on John Cotton in his recent *The Enigma of the Bay Psalm Book* (Chicago, 1956). The best published bibliography of Cotton's writings is that prepared by Julius H. Tuttle in *Bibliographical Essays: A Tribute to Wilberforce Eames* (Privately printed, 1924).

# GODS MERCIE
## MIXED WITH HIS IVSTICE,
### OR,
## HIS PEOPLES DELI-
verance in times of danger.

*Laid open in severall* SERMONS.

By that learned and judicious Divine, and faithfull Minister of JESUS CHRIST JOHN COTTON.

LONDON,
Printed by *G. M.* for *Edward Brewster*, and *Henry Hood* at the Bible on Fleet-Bridge, and in S. *Dunstanes* Church-yard, 1641.

## To the Christian Reader.

Ee read of Elijah that zealous Prophet, that having finished the worke of his great Lord and Master upon earth, he was rapt away by a whirle-winde into Heaven, and left only his mantle behind him, which was preserved by Elisha *as a sacred relique wherewith hee wrought wonders, dividing therewith the waters of* Jordan, 2 King. 2. 11, 13, 14. *Thus the reverend and most learned Authour, another* Elijah, *a faithfull and zealous Prophet, boldly rebuking sinne, frequent, and fervent, and powerfull in prayer, among the people whom the Lord had sent him too; many years together, accounted by some* Ahab-like spirits *an enemy to, and a troubler of* Israel, *which was true of themselves, he being of a most mild and peaceable disposition, maintaining warre onely against the sinnes and corruptions of the times, was at last rapt out of his owne Land into another World, by a terrible whirle-winde of violent opposition raised by Satan and his instruments, through the permission of* God, *and hath onely left his mantle behind him, catch't by some pious* Elisha's, *I meane some broken Notes of his powerfull soule-searching Sermons taken from*

## To the Christian Reader.

his mouth by the diligent hand of some well-disposed hearers and followers, which as they wrought wonders while hee was here dividing betweene many poore soules, and the world and their lusts, and bringing them home to God (wherein scarce any of his Brethren was more successefull) so it's hoped they may tend to the effecting or furthering of the same good worke for the future upon those that shall make use of them: And to that end as some peeces of that Mantle have beene presented to the Church formerly; so some other are heere tendred, which I doubt not but the judicious Christian will kindely accept from the hands of those that have preserved and presented them to their view.

I could say much of the Authour, therby to make you in love with the worke, and not passe the bounds of truth and sobernesse; but the truth is I am too rude a limmer to draw the proportion of him, of his admirable learning, and more admirable graces: It's fit onely to be done by some skilfull Apelles. And besides both the Vniversity, and the place wherein he was setled Pastor many yeares together; yea the whole Land almost, as also divers forraine parts, the Divines whereof some came to enjoy converse with him, others had intercourse with him by letter, have beene acquainted with, and doe retaine in memory his parts and graces; so that (as Paul said of Titus) his praise is in the Gospell, almost throughout all the Churches. Very few that equalled him, scarce any that excelled him in the knowledge of the Arts and Tounges, and in all kinde of learning divine and humane, which made him as a Scribe, instructed unto the Kingdome of Heaven;

## To the Christian Reader.

Heaven; like a good House holder bringing out of his full treasury things new and old, for the comfort and refreshment of Gods family, over which he was set as a dispencer of the mysteries of salvation: and wherby he was inabled in a very great measure to shew himself approoved to God, *a worke-man that needed not to be ashamed, rightly dividing the Word of truth,* as Paul *requires of his beloved* Timothy, 2 Tim. 2. 15. Scarce any of his Brethren were so diligent and painefull in the Lords Harvest, so instant in season, and out of season to preach the word. Neither did he feed his people with the empty huskes of vaine discourses, but he kept the true Patterne of wholesome words, all his Sermons being either Meate to feede, or Medicine to heale his hearers. Neither was he onely a shining light by his Doctrine, but a burning light by his Zealous and holy conversation. His life was, vita vocalis, preaching by his example that Piety, Justice, Sobriety, which he urged in the Pulpit. His actions were, though silent, yet reall Sermons (as Greg. Naz said of Basill.) So that we had cause to cry out for the rapture of this Elijah (*as* Elisha *for that other*) O the Chariots of Israel and the Horsemen thereof! A great part of our strength being lost in him. But our God hath thought good to set him a worke in another part of his vine-yard. Let us therefore make some good use of what wee enjoy of him in these and other of his Sermons.

Good Wine (*saith the* Proverbe) *needs not an* Ivy-bush, Customers enough will finde it out, without a signe: Heere is much good wine, even some of

A 3 those

## To the Christian Reader.

those Flaggons the Spouse desired to be cheared with by her Beloved, Cant. 2. 5. Some of those wines on the lees well refined, Isay. 25. 6. Many sweet and seasonable Doctrines, to refresh the spirits, and to make glad the hearts of Christians, so that had men but a good appetite, were not their soules too full, this work needed not any Ivy bush of commendation to be hung at its doore.

*The Summe of the 1 Sermon, the Title whereof is mistaken.*

Here we have the great love of our God discovered to us, the riches of his patience and goodnesse, and long-suffering, in knocking at the doore of our hearts, and waiting, and suing for entertainment, and promising most sweet and comfortable communion with himselfe, to the soule that opens to him by Faith and Obedience. Never did God knocke louder at the hearts of any people, then at ours, by the exhortations, admonitions, instructions of his faithfull Ministers out of the Pulpit and Presse, by many rare mercies and admirable deliverances, and by opening so faire a doore of hope to us now of freedome from many pressures and corruptions we have groned under, and of becomming a more pure and glorious Church then ever. O let us not make our good God waite any longer in vaine at our doores, but let us heare all his knockes, even that which he gives in the reading of these Sermons, and open to him that we may receive much comfort from him.

*The 2. Sermon.*

Heere wee have also Gods power and mercy laid forth, in delivering his people out of all troubles and tribulations, which they meet with in this vale of teares. Omnis Christianus crucianus, saith Luther, All Christians must be crosse-bearers.

A ll

## To the Christian Reader.

*All* Christophers *that have taken up Christ on the shoulders of their Faith, must wade through a Sea of afflictions, disgraces, oppositions, Persecutions. What a comfort and encouragement is it to be assured that God will make this Ocean fordable and passable to his Saints, that they may goe through it to Heaven, and not be drowned.*

*We have here likewise Gods Mercy to his people shewne by his Iustice to his and their enemies. His love to, and care of the good Corne, in burning up the Bryers and Thornes with the fire of his wrath, that hurted and choaked it, which (if ever) wee see made good among us at present: So as the reading heereof (as a Prophecie fullfilled in our times) may stirre us up to thankfullnesse.*    The 3. Sermon.

*We have here likewise laid open the craft of the wicked, as subtill Foxes to entrap the godly (which the late times have given many sad instances of) by reading whereof those that have avoided their snares may know whom to Blesse for it, even the wisedome and love and care of God over them, and may learne for the future to secke to be furnisht with the wisedome of Christ our Head, that the Pharisees and Sadduces may not prejudice us by their craft and subtilty.*    The 4,5,6. Sermons.

*All these as so many sweete Cups of Wine are heere presented to you, I invite you to taste, yea to drinke aboundantly hereof by serious Meditation and consideration, promising much comfort and benefit to your soules thereby, and requiring the payment of no other shot, then* of your Prayers for the Reverend Authour, and the well-meaning Publishers heereof. Farewell.

From my Study in *London*,
*May* 20, 1641.

Thy Servant for Jesus sake,

MAT. SWALLOWE.

# GODS
## MERCY IN HIS
### Peoples deliverance.

REVEL. 3. 20.

*Behold I stand at the doore and knocke, if any man heare my voyce and open the doore, I will come in to him, and will supp with him, and he with me.*

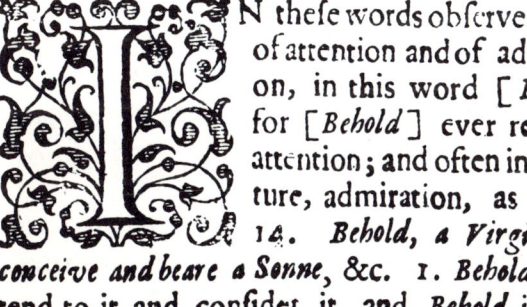

IN these words observe a note of attention and of admiration, in this word [*Behold*] for [*Behold*] ever requires attention; and often in Scripture, admiration, as *Esa.* 7. 14. *Behold, a Virgin shall conceive and beare a Sonne*, &c. 1. *Behold*: Attend to it, and consider it, and *Behold* it with admiration, so heere; *Behold*, consider it well, and stand and wonder that God should *stand at*

B                                                         *the*

*the doore and knocke* there and offer such conditions there, that if any man will open the doore, and hee will enlarge his goodnesse and grace so farre to such, as that he will come in and feast with them.

The first part is a note of attention and admiration, and then the matter to be attended unto what to *behold*.

In the matter of attention, there is,

First, a double act of God, preventing us and going before any care of ours in our turning to God: *Standing and knocking*.

Secondly, a double act of ours, following this double act of God. Heare my voyce, *Open the doore*.

Thirdly, Behold also a double act of God, that follows this double act of ours, *I will come in unto him, and supp with him:* I Feast with him, and be feasted of him: These be the parts.

A necessary counsell and charge to all the people of God, that live in a Church subject to lukewarmenesse, that have some affections stirred up, but with much want of fervency and life of grace.

This whole verse may bee fitly opened to you in opening three principall notes, carrying an end the sence of the whole Scripture.

First, when our Saviour saith, *Behold I stand at the doore and knocke*, &c. Wee are first to enquire, what this doore is, which wee shall see in this one Doctrine.

*That*

*That the heart of a man is the doore of the* **Doct.**
*soule.*

The heart is the way of the entrance of God into the soule, or into the whole man: For, when the Holy Ghost will give us an example of this very thing of the opening of the *doore*, speaking of *Lydia*, he expresseth it thus, *whose heart the Lord opened*, *Acts* 16. 14. the doore to be opened, was the heart of *Lydia*, that was it, at which Christ *stood and knocked*, and that she opened unto him, and so *Psal.*24.7,9. *Bee yee lift up you everlasting doores*, and what are those doores: but the hearts of men? They are not the doores of a mans house, nor the gates of a city, for they will bee consumed, but these be everlasting doores, and such as into which the *king of Glory must enter*, and they must be inlarged, this is certainely meant of the heart of man, and of the will of man which dwels in the heart.

Now for the Reason, why the heart is called the doore: for you might say, if the heart of a man be the doore of the soule, what is the inward chaire of the soule, what is more inward, then the heart of a man? Satan can tell what is in a mans fancy and many times what is in a mans heart that hee knowes not, if there be any secret in a man it is in his heart and will: Why is it then that he cals the most inmost closet of the soule, the doore of the soule?

It is called the doore of the soule, because **Reason.**
of

of that authority that the heart and will hath over the whole soule, and the power it hath to rule both soule and body. As in cities, the strength of the city is in the gates, there was their Seates of Iustice in those dayes, and there was munition stored up for war, so that open the gates to an enemy, and you give him all, this commands all; give the heart of a man, and you have a free passage into the whole man, if a man get the gates of a city, he hath all: So give God the heart, and then you give him the whole soule and body too, *Iohn* 10. 7, 9. *I am the doore, by me if any man enter hee shall be saved:* Take Christ, and you take salvation with him: you take Heaven with you, and all the blessings of God at once, that if hee be opened unto you, there is nothing denied you, of all the living treasures of the grace of God, have him, and you have a strong entrance into your owne salvation, have him and you have a good calling to any personall estate, in Family, Church or commonwealth: so in this respect our Saviour cals the heart of a man the doore; give God the heart, and you give him authority over your whole soule, in the whole course of your life. And therefore God saith, *Prov.* 23. 26. *My sonne give me thy heart*; as if a Prince lying before the gates of a city, give him the gates, and you resigne your selves in subjection to such a Prince, and so is it heere.

*Vse.* It doth shew you how farre short wee are from giving God any possession within us, any hold of us

*Gods mercy in his Peoples deliverance,*

us, as long as wee content our selves with any measures of knowledge and grace, and doe not change and open the heart: If that a man were filled with all the treasures of knowledge and wisedome, and fully inlightned in his minde and judgement, so as hee may know the whole body of the Scriptures, and if God have this, and onely this, hee hath yet nothing, *he stands at the doore:* yea if this man should come off with many good affections, sometimes with griefe for sinne; and sometimes trembling at the word; and sometimes joy in hearing; as *Herod* rejoyced in *Iohns* Doctrine; and *Ahab* grieved at the threatning, and *Felix* trembled, and *Iehu* was zealous in executing the word of the Lord, and yet God had as yet no part in any of them: Christ stood yet without doores, and had no part in *Herod*, *Ahab* or *Iehu*, &c. no place within them, yet if a man were as forward as *Herod* to reforme many things, *Mark.* 6.20. yet if Christ have not the heart, hee hath nothing. And therefore this calleth upon us all, never to rest in any beginnings of grace, nor in any measures of grace whatsoever they bee, untill God have the heart, till our wils receive and imbrace him, and so open to him, that hee may come in conquering to conquer, and in subduing to subdue, our judgements and passions, and affections and speeches, that God may passe through our whole man freely without disturbance, till then God hath nothing: It is true you may give a Prince the gates of a City, and yet hee may finde disturbance

bance and battle in the market place; and so it is with many of the servants of God, though wee have given the heart to God, and hee hath taken possession thereof with some entrance into the whole man, yet when hee comes to meete with us in this and that businesse wherein our affections are most stirring, there is some way or other, some insurrections made against God. Many times worldly busines and strength of lusts may oppose much; but if indeed God have our hearts given him, then though hee have worke enough with us, to subdue our pride and worldlinesse and wantonnesse, and other distempers in us, hee shall have something to doe when hee comes to these passages wherein nature is more stirring, many skirmishes there will bee against God, but if wee have once given God the heart, in time hee will have all, and though hee meete with many skirmishes, yet hee will prevaile in the end: so that let not men satisfie themselves in giving God any part of their lives in the whole course of their conversation, or any affections, but give him the heart, and when hee hath that then hee will take the rest, with-hold that and give him all the rest, and hee makes account you give him nothing.

Come wee then to the second point, and to speake more fully of that,

*Doctrine 2.* *The patience and bounty of God is great towards sinners, even admirable great in calling them home to himselfe.*

It is worthy all admiration to behold this patience

ence of God. This is expreſt in the two firſt acts of God; it is very great patience of God, that he will ſtand and waite upon us, it is not a word of courſe that is there uſed to fill up the ſentence, but it expreſſeth that in which we would expreſſe our patience, if wee ſtood at a mans doore from day to day, and from weeke to weeke with ſtrong deſires to enter into it, is not that patience? And therefore when hee ſaith, *I ſtand*, it argues the patience of God.

And this argues his bounty too, that hee not onely ſtands there, but hee uſes vehement and effectuall meanes to bee heard, and ſuch meanes as by which hee might make way for opening to himſelfe: Firſt, for Gods patience that this is done by God in calling us home to him, that is the very ſcope of our Saviour in this Text.

And for his ſtanding at the *doore*, ſee his Patience in that *Rom.* 10. 21. *All the day long have I ſtretched out my hand*, &c. it was a long ſtanding, and that day is not meant a naturall or artificiall day, but a long ſeaſon of grace, *Luke* 13. 7. *Theſe three yeares have I ſtayed and looked for fruite*, three yeers God ſtaied for it, Yea, you reade, *Pſalm.* 95. 10. God complaines, *Fourty yeeres long was I grieved with this generation*: Fourty yeers God ſometimes ſtayes before hee will threaten, *that they ſhall never enter into his reſt*: yea yet longer; *My Spirit ſhall not alwaies ſtrive with man, Gen.* 6. 3. 5. the ſonnes of God, the beſt of mankinde are become fleſh; yet his dayes ſhall be an hundred and twenty yeares, hee will ſtay for that generation before

fore hee bring the flood an hundred and twenty yeares.

But that I may more fully expresse to you the patience of God in staying thus for us, let mee shew you it in 4. particulars.

1. First, in staying long before hee doe take any notice of sinne, hee saith nothing though wee sinne, and continue in sinne, and multiply transgressions against him day after day, and yeare after yeare: God takes no notice of any thing wee doe, but carries it, as if he saw it not, and heard it not, *Psal*, 50.20,21. *I held my tongue and said nothing:* I stayed so long as that thou thoughtest I did approve of thy evill courses, he thinks God lookes at him now, as hee did twenty or thirty, or fourty, or an hundred yeares agoe, and hee never found checke in his soule for what hee had done, nor any judgement of God upon him in any remarkable manner, so as hee thinkes hee hath done no evill.

2. Secondly, another act of his patience is not onely a holding his peace so long, but when he doth beginne to stirre, hee doth alwayes usually threaten before hee strike, *Amos* 4.11,12. *because I will doe thus unto thee O Israel, prepare to meet thy God,* hee usually threatens before hee strikes: hee seldome doth strike, at least irrecoverably, till hee give men warning.

3. Thirdly, when hee threatens, hee will not yet strike, but will yet stay a good time after he hath threatned, *Hos.* 11.7,8,9. *My bowels are turned within me for thee,* so that God when hee is about to

to strike, it comes into his minde, how shall I doe it, what would become of thee, if I should take this course with thee, and so leave thee hopelesse and helpelesse for after time.

Fourthly, he doth not onely so; but suppose he doe strike (as usually he doth) in the end, if all this prevaile not, yet see how long hee stands, hee doth with-draw his blow when hee hath stricken, he doth not stirre up all his wrath, but with-holds the fiercenesse of his displeasure, at least for a good time, and rather gives warning then breaks forth in his full displeasure, *Psf.* 78.38. *Many a time he turned his anger away and did not stirre up all his wrath*; Hee did expresse his displeasure, and sometimes afflicted some of them, and sometimes others of them; but did not consume them utterly: See it in the example of *Davids* carriage to *Saul*, when hee cut off the skirt of his garment, hee might as well have cut off his life: So *Saul* when hee was riding to *Damascus*, to destroy all them that called on the name of the Lord Iesus, Christ meetes him, and strikes him downe to the ground, and strucke him blinde; hee might as easely have strucke him dead, and so hath done many, *Act.* 9.4,8. The same stroke that strucke him to the ground, might have strucke him into the grave, and from thence into the nethermost hell, but where had then beene all *Pauls* gratious Epistles and glorious sufferings, and therefore well may wee say, God was willing to shew an example of long-suffering towards him, else when God had strucke him downe hee would have there have let him lyen, and not let him rise againe and given him leave to heare more good counsell, that hee might turne to God, and become a new man, as hee did, which shews you the wonderfull patience of God before he fall upon a creature in the utmost of his displeasure.

Secondly, Behold also the bounty of God towards poore sinners, when he cals them home to him: *I stand at the doore and knocke*, that expresseth some vehement urging that sinners might open to him.

Now what are these stroakes of God by which hee doth expresse this knocking?

1. First, he strikes with the hammer of his word, as many doores have hammers hanging at them, that make a shrill and a loud noyse, that will waken men though they were asleepe; so God compares his Word to an hammer, *Ier.* 23. 29. Sometimes, puts such weight upon his Word, that the Word spoken by the Ministers of God, to the hearts and consciences of men, rings a loud noyse in the eares of men; so as afterwards they cannot eat, nor sleep for thinking of the sad noyse that word did ring in their ears.

2. But 2. He knockes also by his judgements, and knockes a loud; there is not any sickenesse befalls us or ours, not any losse in our estates, not any kind of evill that befals the places where we live, so farre as it reaches us: but it is a knocke of Gods hand to turne to him, *Acts* 16. 26.

When

When the Earth was smitten with a great earthquake, so as that the prison doores were opened, and the power of God in them both did shake the heart of the Gaoler, that out of bed hee leapes, and to the prison hee comes, and there had like to have slaine himselfe, fearing the Prisoners had beene fled; but seeing none of them was run away, it pleased God so to strike in with that stroake, that hee presently fals downe and cries out; *Sirs, what must I doe to bee saved?* When a judgement comes and makes the foundations of a mans heart to shake, it sets his spirit a trembling, and puts him into a feare, so awakened with the power of God, expressed in some Iudgement, that hee knowes not what to doe. You know how mightily God *knocked* at *Pharaohs* heart, when as in sundry of the latter judgements, the Text saith, *That he sends for* Moses *in haste, and confesseth that the Lord is righteous, and that he had sinned,* and comes off very seriously, as if he would now wholy yeeld to Gods will, though before hee had said, who is the Lord, such a mighty power is in the judgements of God.

3. Thirdly, There is another voyce of God that knocks, and God in that shewes much bounty; and that is when God is pleased to knocke at the doores of our hearts by the worke of his Spirit; by opening our conscience, which is as a fortresse before the doores of our hearts; as in many great cities there are some out-workes to defend the gates; God so convinces the

C 2 con-

conscience, and inlightens the minde, and informes the judgement, and the memory and affections; so as that all the out-workes of the soule are subdued, whereby it comes to passe they professe to God that if hee will but spare them to a certaine further time, they will doe whatsoever God commands them; this many times fals out, that God takes hold of the minde and judgement and conscience, and affections, so as nothing stands out but onely the very doore, the heart is onely shut, *Iohn* 16.9. *They are convinced of sinne, of righteousnesse and of judgement*, which argues that the Spirit of God when hee comes, he will inlighten the minde, and convince the judgement, and let the world plainely see that their way is wrong, and that they are yet in a damnable estate, because they beleeve not in him; this is one of the strongest knocks of God, when the minde and judgement is convinced, and the heart ready to condemne it selfe, and acknowledge that if it should now stand out any longer, the case would proove dangerous. And when God takes this paines, is there not a plentifull expression of his bounty to us.

Fourthly, There is onely one stroake more which God many times doth follow the rest withall, and alwayes doth when hee intends to knocke prevailingly, and it is this: Hee doth many times breake open the doore of the heart, though wee bee unready and unlisty to open, hee lets fall in some savour of the Lord Iesus, and

and some relish of the Spirit of Adoption, *Cant.* 5.4,5. that though the heart bee drowsie and dead in sinne, yet it begins to arise and open to Christ; and then though Christ bee gone, yet the heart runnes after him, and though shee cannot of a long time finde him, yet shee continues to seeke him; and this is when the Spirit of Adoption hath made it a broken heart.

Now, why should God bee thus wonderfull patient and bountifull in standing and knocking at the doors of our hearts?

The first and principall reason is taken from God himselfe, and it is from the purpose he hath to glorifie the riches of his mercy and grace to poor sinners, notable is that speech, and remember it for ever, & let it sink deep into your hearts like Myrrh which may preserve your savour, *Esa.* 30.18. Therfore will the Lord wait that hee may be gracious to us: This is the first Reason, why God will thus waite and stand and knocke, and tarry our leisure, that hee might exalt the glory of his rich grace towards us, if the King or some great man should stand waiting long at our doore, if hee should stand ten, twenty or an hundred yeers, you would thinke he debased himselfe, to stand waiting so long on such wretches as wee are; but Gods thoughts are not like mans, when hee waits long; it is that hee might bee gracious, and hee will bee exalted in so doing: waiting and exalting is put, the one to expresse the other: They interpret

*Reaso.*

and

and expound one another, to magnifie the riches of his patience, hee will waite and not bee weary of waiting, sometimes for some scores of yeeres together, and indeed God is not disappointed, for such hee will prevaile with in his own time to open to him, 1 *Tim.* 1.14,16,17. *The grace of God was exceeding aboundant towards me, I was a blasphemer and injurious, a persecutor* &c. *but the grace of God was exceeding aboundant towards me,* and hee tels you wherein God shewed forth his long sufferance to me, as a pattern of all those that should afterwards beleeve: And see how he ends that speech, *vers* 17. *Now to the King immortall, to the onely wise God be power and glory for ever.* Thus you see what this waiting of God wrought, hee waites and knockes that hee might bee exalted in that day; that when they see, what a dangerous estate they are in, and yet see how patiently God hath forborne them, and bountifully expressed himself towards them, and see in the end God hath broken in upon them, and will no longer stand: then this grace was exceeding aboundant towards me, and now God is exalted: the mouth is for ever after open to Gods praise.

2 *Reason* taken from the will and purpose of God for the salvation of our soules. God is not slacke, when hee is so slow in powring out his devouring judgements, but patient to us ward, (2 *Pet.*3.9.) who would have no man to perish, but all men to come to repentance: this is the Reason why hee is thus patient, and **long-suffering**, that we might
not

not perish, but might come to the knowledge of his will: if God were not patient towards us all, and knocked but once or twice, wee had beene crushed into the nethermost hell, where had all his glorious Saints in Heaven, and all his gracious servants in Earth beene, if hee had not beene a patient, and bountifull God; but hee is not willing we should perish. Every child of God had perished and that everlastingly, had not God magnified his patience toward them. He did not stirre up all his wrath, Becauſe, *Hee remembred we were but flesh, a blast of wind that goes away, and returnes not againe*, *Pſal*.78.38,39. as if he should say, if God when wee provoke his patience, and stand out long against him, should then stirre up all his wrath, wee should have no hope to turne to God, for wee are but dust, blowne away and returne not againe. If God strike a man with death, what hope is there that hee shall returne againe: where had *Paul* beene if hee had beene strucke to death as well as to the earth, hee had never returned then to have seene the light of the living. God therefore that considers what sorry things wee bee, and that if hee should but stirre up all his wrath, wee should bee utterly undone, hee will therefore stay many yeers, before he poure out all his wrath, and utterly consume us. *Reaſon* 3.

Hee waites and knockes long to leave all flesh without excuſe that will not turne to Him, *Rom*.1. 20. ſpeaking of ſuch as had but the light of nature, yet men are left without excuſe, that they do *Reaſon* 4.

doe not acknowledge God, and glorifie him as God, how much more when hee endures with long patience, and such loud and vehement knocking at the hearts of men; and sometimes by taking the out-workes of the soule, the minde and judgement, and affections, &c. he will leave men without excuse, if after all this they will stand out against him.

*Vse* 1. To leade us to Repentance, *Rom*.2.4,5. it is a pregnant place to this purpose; *Despisest thou the patience and bounty, and long-sufferance of God*, &c. See what vehement reasons the Apostle useth to perswade and urge us to take advantage heereby to turne unto God by Repentance. See how hee glorifies these attributes of God by casting shame upon us, if wee repent not. *Despisest thou*, who speakes hee of? Hee speakes to the *Romanes*, the great Lords of the world at that day, for none of the Nations were like unto them, for prowesse and government and authority and yet despisest thou? Thou *Romane*, what thou that hast beene exalted above all Nations, thou whom God hath so highly advanced and adorned with all manner of excellencies, as if hee should say; Thou: Who art thou, or what art thou at the best, who art thou that thou shouldest despise the bounty of God, thou whom God hath brought up from so meane a condition, is it for thee to stand contesting with God; let mee tell thee whoever thou beest, it is not for mortall men, dust and ashes, a blast to despise the patience and bounty of God; so that the Apostle
doth

doth strongly presse this duty of Repentance by an argument taken from the patience and bounty of God. How therefore should this awaken the heart of every one that heares mee this day, call every (thou) every one of your soules by name, and say, what thou, whom God hath beene so patient too, twenty, thirty, fourty, an hundred yeers (Thou) whom hee hath visited with so much sickenesse, (Thou) whom God hath brought from a meane condition, to a large measure of estate, (Thou) whom God hath beene thus patient too; *despisest thou the patience of God?* presse this upon your hearts, and abuse his patience no longer.

And consider another argument. The bountie and long sufferance of God; consider your danger, hee intends to terrifie the heart of the most stubborne sinner, with what hee speakes in *verse 5. Thou treasurest up wrath against the daie of wrath, Treasurest up wrath*, there is not a man that stands out the patience of God, but this is his case, *he treasures up wrath against the day of wrath*. A treasure consists not in trifles and sorry things, though a man have store of them, treasures are choise things, and variety and store of such things makes a treasure: Now what would the Apostle awake the heart to see and know? that a man that doth despise the patience and bounty of God, hee doth procure to himselfe speciall, rare, choyse and extraordinary wrath and judgement, not onely one or two, but variety, choise and store, upon body, soule and conscience,

D

science upon children and estate left behinde. And therefore suffer the word of Exhortation, and receive this counsell from the Apostle, and that to your hearts, if you doe not turne to God, when hee thus turnes to you, you will bee upbraided by God, *despisest thou*; or else the wrath of God, will in the end be treasured up in such rare and singular judgements upon you, that hee that heares of it, both his eares shall tingle; Neighbours and Friends shall stand amazed to see the woefull judgements that befals thee: Now therefore delay the time no longer, despise Gods patience no more; treasure up no more wrath, there is enough gone out already, but even now turne to God with all thy heart.

*Vse* 2. To teach sinners not utterly to despaire, though sometimes they have stood out long against God; for God is indeed patient and long-suffering, hee stands and that very long: You see what paines hee takes, and still stands to see if wee will open to him; and therefore let no man be discouraged, what if thou hast staied three yeers, what if fourty, what if a hundred and twenty yeers, yet all this time God hath stayed; let it not now hinder thee from turning to God, for feare hee should despise thee, or so much wrath belongs to thee, as is mercilesse. It is true, men may justly so feare, but as long as God waites, and especially so long as hee knockes, there is some hope, if thou wilt but open there is hope.

But

But you say, how shall I know that God stands knocking? If a man bee growne old in sinne, and his conscience seared as with an hot yron: that hee descerns not a knocke of God in his heart, then time is past with him. But as long as God stands and knocks, so long hee ha h a mind to enter.

But how shall I know whether hee knocke or no?

Doth God hammer thy conscience, and all as upon an Anvell, the case is dangerous; but if God strike and thou feelest it, there is yet hope, or if some judgement befall thee, say it bee some inward anguish of soule, and doth it bring thee down and set thee a wrastling for grace, now God is a knocking: And if thou findest the Lord convincing thy conscience and possesse thy minde and judgement of the danger of thy estate, and if thou seest out of the Word, that God is now a laying siege to thy soule, surprizing the out-works thereof, accusing and condemning thy conscience, all this while there is hope in *Israel*, unlesse thou at length provoke God to further wrath, yet God waites still, that he may be gracious to exalt his mercy, and the aboundant riches of his grace and his long-sufferance; therefore bee not discouraged, but now take opportunity, least thou goe on to despise and seale up wrath against thee.

*Vse* 3. To teach all those who have had experience of this patience and bounty of God, leading you to repentance, and have found comfort in it, now live cheerfully and magnifie the rich Name of the Lord Jesus, and his glorious bounty, and hold it foorth as a patterne to all about thee, that thou hast stood out so long against so many warnings and expressions and manifestations of Gods bounty, since that is the end God aymes at, let now his name and his great patience and bounty bee magnified and speake of it from one generation to another, that the memory of it may not dye.

*Doctrine 3.* *Such as doe heare the voyce and knocks of Christ and doe open the doore of their hearts to him, hee will vouchsafe fellowship with them, familiar and continuall fellowship with them, feasting of them and be feasted by them.*

To heare the voyce of Christ, is to heare it with a boared eare, and with regard and reverence, hee so heares, as hee never forgets what God speaks, he hears with an everlasting ear, *Iam.*1.24,25,26. *Mine ears hath God opened, Psa.*40.6. God hath digged into a mans ears (so it is in the Originall) so *Esa.*50.4,5. *The Lord hath opened mine eare, so that I was not rebellious nor turned backe*, *Iohn* 6.45. hee heares with an everlasting eare, it is a sound that never goes out of his eare, whether God speake to him in his Word, or in his judgements, or by the voyce of his Spirit in his heart and conscience, hee hath heard the voyce of his rod, *Micah* 6.9. this is hearing with a digged eare: Such an hearing as *David* saith, *I will never forget thy precepts, Psalme* 119.

But

But how then are wee said to open the doore?

By these severall acts.

First, We open to Christ, when wee beleeve all that God hath spoken: for wee may heare and understand much, but our hearts beleeve it not, and then we doe not open the doore of faith, and so doe not open our hearts, if wee open the heart wee give up our hearts to God to imbrace whatever hee hath spoken, *Act.* 14. 27. Wee beleeve the truth of the Word, and give credence and have assurance of the certainty and goodnesse of it to our souls, when we are able to say, good is the Word of the LORD, this is the key of Faith.

Secondly, Wee open the doore of our hearts, when wee goe to God and openly confesse from our hearts all the despight and contempt we have put Gods grace too, when wee in confession open the mouth and the heart together, and confesse that all God hath spoken to us of our dangerous course, hath beene the Word of his truth and goodnesse, when wee confesse former and latter sins, and judge our selvs as unworthy of any mercy, he that thus confesseth and forsaketh his sins shall find mercy, *Pro.* 28. 13. he that keepes his heart fast lockt, hee keepes out God, and hardens his heart from good counsell, hee shall fall into mischiefe, and for him there is no remedy, *Prov.* 29. 1. but if wee confesse our sinne unto God; this is the way to soften and open the heart.

Third-

Thirdly, If wee have made God stay long before wee open to him, this will further be found: Wee open our hearts, when as wee desire to give up our hearts and soules to God, not onely to receive him and his grace, but even to yeelde professed subjection to the Gospell of Christ; when our hearts professe, it is too long that wee have stood out so many knockes, but now for time to come, we yeeld and offer our soules to God, not to leave an hoofe behind; but now Christ shall have minde and judgement and conscience, all our indeavours, all that wee are or can bee, 2 *Cor.* 9.13. when wee yeeld every thought to professed subjection to Christ and his Gospell, when wee will not allow our selves in any passage of sinne, but yeeld up our selves, soules and bodies and spirits and all to bee guided by him, to doe and suffer his will, that we may be delivered from the wrath to come.

Now suppose we do thus, what will God then do to us?

Why Christ will vouchsafe familiar communion with us, hee will come in and dwell with us; to dwell with a man is to continue with him, and to grow to more familiar fellowship with him, give him your heart, and then he will never depart from you, *Ier.* 32.40.

*He will sup with us, and we with him.*

That implyes still more familiar communion with him.

Wee are said to *sup* with God: First, when he doth

doth refresh us, set before us the fat things of his grace, set before us the Lord Iesus Christ, and gives us his holy Spirit, set before us peace of conscience, and joy in the Holy Ghost, and all the gifts and graces of his Spirit, invites us to his Ordinances, and sets before us the comfort of them.

1 He gratiously invites us to his Ordinances, 2 and there sets before us Christ and his benefits, 3 and then at supper time hee carves us out some choise portion reserved for us, he gives us a testimony of our welcome in the dishes of his ordinances, and in the meate in them Christ, and in the benefits hee carves out to us, he saith, here is a part for thee sonne or daughter, here is not a dish upon the Table, but thou hast thy part in it, God will so take order, not one benefit of Christ Iesus, not a Sermon, not a Sacrament, not a blessing in Christian communion, but there is something in them to feed thee, and therefore see thou be strengthened and comforted in them, and built up by them, there is nothing but something is for thee, no promise but its thine, no Commandement but it belongs to thee, no example but for your good and imitation, and then are we said to sup with him.

But when is hee said to suppe with us?

1. When hee will be present with us in every duty, when hee shewes us his presence and 2. assistance in every performance, and when hee not onely shewes his presence and assistance, but is pleased 3. to accept this and that duty, we
offer

offer him our service, and indeavours and desires, whereby wee bid him welcome to our house, and then hee shews us his acceptance of our duties, it is our meate and drinke to performe Christian duties in a Christian manner, when you little think that God takes notice of them, yet hee accepts it all. And,

First, Christ will rejoyce in us. Secondly, some poore Christians that joyne with us shall be glad to heare of such expressions come from us; the loynes and bowels of poore Christians shall be refreshed, and it shall bee as much comfort to them, as if you had layed a good morsell upon his trencher. And all from this; because wee have heard Christs voyce and opened unto him; if there bee first a willing mind it is accepted, 2 *Cor.* 8.12. If God give us grace to performe any poore duty with a willing mind, hee accepts it, this is the best entertainement we had for him, and the best courses wee can take, we could wish our entertainement were better for him; but it is sufficient, for it is accepted.

*Vse* 1. It is of Exhortation to all that never knew what it was to sit downe at table with God, this is commended to you; *If any man will heare my voyce, if he will but open the doore I will come in to him*, dost thou desire to bee entertained at the Lords Table, or when thou commest to any ordinance of God, wouldest thou have the Lord Iesus Christ to bid thee wellcome, this is the course that is commended to thee, set open an everlasting eare to hearken what this day is
spo-

spoken to thee, confider all the good counfell God hath given you out of his Word, *harden not your hearts as in the day of provocation*, let none of the feeds of Gods word fall to the ground in vain, but what you have once heard, heare it for ever, *Hebr.* 2.1,2. You have this day heard of the great patience and rich grace and large bounty of God, let not the word of his grace fall to the ground in vaine, call it to minde and beleeve the truth of it, and in beleeving of it profeffe your hearts to God in an hearty confeffion, that indeede you have ftood out long againſt him, and againſt all his bounty, and truth, befeech him to breake open the ſtony doores of your heart, and burſt the barrs of Iron in afunder, and to give you an heart to give up your foule and body and fpirit to him, which is a reafonable ferving of him, give up minde and judgement and affection to God; and if you finde your hearts fluggiſh this way, remember on the one fide, *You will treafure up wrath againſt the day of wrath*, if you doe not: and if you doe fo, then Chriſt will come in and *ſuppe with you*, taking in good part, what you performe, and making you a continuall feaſt, *Prov.*15.15. and others ſhall rejoyce in your behalfe, and this will be a fupper to you; you ſhall need no more nor better meate, till you goe to your everlaſting long home, having gotten fuch a fupper you may then goe to bed when you will, and you ſhall ſleepe moſt ſweetly and comfortably, in another world hee will make his laſt meale with you, when your eyes ſhall clofe up in everlaſting

lasting peace, remember this and make use of it for ever.

*Vse* 2. To teach the servants of Christ that have sometimes supt with him heeretofore, if you have not found Christ, carving out a portion to you of a long time, it is a direction to you as you would have Christ present with you, and his acceptance in al your duties, it behoves you so often as you come before God, come with a boared care, that every word may sink deep into you; and know that the reason why Christ was not present with you, in publik or in private, was, because you either have not heard or not opened to him, you have not beleived, not confessed your miscariages, not yeelded to God your after-course, and hence you have come to duties, and neither your selves nor others better for them; set therfore open your hearts to Christ, and heare his voyce, and give up your selves to bee wholy taught of God for time to come, and then hee will readily accept you, and will carve you out a blessing out of every ordinance you come to; and you shall finde this verified, hee will keepe a feast with you this night, and the last night you sleepe, shall bee sweet to you, and you shall awake with comfort at the resurrection of the just.

## FINIS.

# THE SAINTS DELIVERANCE OVT OF TRIbulations.

R E V, 7, latter patt of the 14, ver.
*These are they which came out of great tribulation, and have washed their robes and made them white in the blood of the Lambe.*

From the ninth verse of this Chapter you have a description of Gods Church and people that obtained victory and deliverance out of a great danger which lay upon themselves, and the whole Church of God; the judgement and danger is expressed in *verse* 1, 2. Their preservation by the

seale

seale of God set upon them is exprest from verse 3. to the 8.

In the ninth verse you have a description of the persons preserved and so delivered.

First, as *Iohn* did perceive them to bee by his owne view and hearing, *I beheld*, &c.

Secondly, as hee did learne them to be by the information of one of the Angels. As hee perceived them by his own discerning, hee describes them.

1. First, for multitude, a *great multitude*, so great as none could number them.

2. Secondly, for their country and the variety of them, *They were of all people and nations and languages*.

3. Thirdly, for their place, *they were before the throne*, which appeares from *verse* 4. had a place in the Church.

4. Fourthly, he discernes them by their habit, *ver. 9. cloathed with white robes and palmes in their hands*.

5. Fiftly, He describes them, as he sees them to be by their imployment, what he heard or saw them do, *they cryed out with a loud voyce*, and hee tels you what it was, and how it was confirmed by the testimony of all the Angels of God: Their preservation in evill and deliverance out of inward and outward evils they ascribe it all to God, *that sits upon the throne*, and to the *Lambe*. All the while that the judgement lay upon the earth, many of Gods people were carried to this false conceit and misconceiving of God and themselves,

in ascribing salvation to themselves, too much respect had they to their owne works and merits, but after God had beene pleased to wash them in the blood of his sonne, they saw now that salvation from death and sinne and affliction, was from him that *sits upon the throne,* and the Temple and from the Lamb, the blood of Christ.

This confirmed by all the Angels. *ver.* 11, 12. *They cryed and said, blessing and glory and wisdome &c. be unto our God for ever.*

And then hee comes to describe them in the Verse before the Text, and in the Text, hee describes them, by what hee learned of them by information, and that from one of the *Elders* that stood by and shewed him these things.

The *Elder* enquires first of him, to prepare him the better to understand it: *Knowest thou what these be?* *John* returnes an answer of his ignorance, and likewise an expression of his desire after information; thou knowest and art likely to know it: who then returnes him this answer, that they that thus stand with ensignes of victory, *These are they which came out of great tribulation, and have washed their robes in the blood of the Lamb.*

So then you have in these words a description of the estate of Gods people by a double argument.

First, by their deliverance out of affliction from great tribulations.

Secondly, by their profiting under affliction, which *have washed their robes and made them white in the blood of the Lambe.*

These

These are not a description of the Saints glorified in Heaven, though it bee true of them, but hee speakes heere of the servants of God upon Earth, for in the *verse* following it is said, *They are such as serve God day and night in the Temple*, which in Heaven men are not said to doe, there is no Temple there to serve God in; but it is ment of the servants of God in earth, described as you heard before.

These two particulars yeeld two doctrines.

Doctrine 1. *The tribulations of Gods people are sometimes great and deepe, but alwayes safe and passable.*

*Great and deepe*, great and deepe tribulations, sore afflictions they were exercised with, but even then safe and passable. These are they that are come out of their great tribulations, they are preserved in them, and safely delivered out of them, and now they tryumph in the Church of God with the presence of the Lamb of God, and sing Psalmes to his praise. It was the earnest supplication of Christ our Saviour to his Father, *Mat.* 26.39. *If it be possible let this cuppe passe from mee,* his earnest desire was that the great tribulation he was then entering upon, which caused him to sweate clods of water and blood, and made him cry out, *God had forsaken him*, hee desires that it might be a passable tribulation, that hee might not bee swallowed up of it, nor over-whelmed by it, and hee was heard in the thing which hee prayed for, *Hebr.*5.7. so as that this great tribulation, greater then which never any creature suffered, this cuppe passed from him, it did not o-
ver-whelme

ver-whelme him: And as it was with Christ the head, so it is with all his members, what ever cup the Father mixes for us to drinke, when wee have drunke of it, it passeth from us, it doth not make us drunken as the cuppe given to *Babylon* did, their affliction did so over-whelme them that they were the worse for it ever after; but Gods peoples affliction is passing great, and many (for so the word signifies, *Psal.*34.19.) are the troubles of the righteous, but the Lord delivers them out of them all, be they never so many and great, *yet the Lord delivers them out of them all,* they are all of them safe in the bottome and in the issue, and all of them passable, *Psal.* 40.2. *Hee brought me out of the horrible pit, out of the horrible pit of the grave and hell, out of the miery clay, where he could finde no bottome, and set him upon a rocke,* and then hee found a bottome, though there was no bottome at the first to be found to his feeling, yet hee found safety in it and a good issue out of it, *Psal,*71.20. *Thou which hast shewed me great and sore troubles shalt quicken me againe, and shalt bring me againe from the depths of the Earth:* Suppose a man were fallen into deepe afflictions, and lay under great and sore troubles, yet thou wilt revive mee, and lift me up from thence, this God will doe, though the Apostle sometimes say wee are in despaire, hee was troubled out of measure, and had received the sentence of death in it selfe, but hee hath delivered us from so great a death, there is great tribulation, and that brings great death, and great
feare

feare of death, which put him to great paine and anguish, and yet out of this the Lord delivered him.

You have some famous examples in Scripture that stand as guides in the way, to give light to them that passe by, what great afflictions Gods servants have beene in, and yet preserved in them and delivered out of them: *Daniel* in the Lyons denne, the three children in *Nebuchadnezzars* fiery furnace, *Dan.3.6*. Famous is the story of *Ionah* in the whales belly; such examples as these, stand as Monuments of this truth, these are they which come out of great tribulations: Thus *Ionah* and *Daniel* and others like unto them that have beene in great and sore dangers, when in the gates of death, and the waves have overwhelmed them in the gulph of destruction: yet God hath called them from thence, and lift them up and delivered them. The *Ægyptian* darkenesse which Gods people suffered in the house of bondage: The *Babylonian* captivity in which the people of God were a type of that great captivity, partly of sinne, which Gods people are subject to be drawne too, and partly of bondage, which the Church of God under Antichrist were likely to endure, they both expresse what the Church of God felt; now from all these it pleased God to redeeme them, and put songs of salvation into their mouthes, and Palmes of victories into their hands.

*Reason* 1.   *Reas.* 1. From the fellowship which Gods people have with Christ Jesus in his death and resurrection,

rection, that is the first and principall ground, and often shall you reade it, *Col.* 2.10. *Wee are dead and risen with Christ*: If Iesus Christ the *Lamb of God*, if hee die and rise againe from the dead, all his people shall have a time at one time or another to bring them as low as the grave, and yet out of the grave shall they rise againe; for the death and resurrection of Christ is a pledge of a three-fold death and resurrection in us.

First, in that wee are dead in sinne, wee shall rise from that.

Secondly, though dead to the grave, yet wee shall also rise from thence.

Thirdly, dead in afflictions, yet wee shall rise out of them all, none of all those evils that Gods people are subject too, be it sinne or the grave or affliction, and what ever else; by the death of Christ wee die to all these, and by his resurrection, wee rise againe out of them all; there is no evill wee can fall into, but hee that raised up Christ from the dead shall also quicken us, from sinne, the grave, hell, and from all afflictions: *Timothy* was a yong Souldier of Iesus Christ, and *Paul* that was more beaten to that warfare, when hee encourages him to suffer as a good Souldier, hee bids him remember that *Iesus Christ was risen from the dead*, 2 *Timothy* 2.3,8. Do you thinke it is likely that such a great and eminent servant of God, as *Timothy* was, should forget that Christ was risen againe; why truely wee doe forget it, as often as wee are discouraged with afflictions, but therefore that hee might incourage Christians to looke at all afflictions as dead matter, as

F　　　　　　　　　already

already crucified, looke wee at all tribulations, and doe but remember that Chrift was dead and is rifen againe, and it will bee a ground for our Faith, when ever wee come into affliction.

*Reafon 2.*    *Reafon* 2. That (which flowes from hence) and it is taken from that great redemption, which the Lord Iefus by his death and refurrection hath wrought for us. Wee have fellowfhip with him in his death and refurrection, and from hence comes *plentious redemption*, *Pfa.*130.7,8. fo that if there be plentious Redemption in Chrift, then though our tribulations be great and plentifull and deepe, yet with the Lord is plentious redemption. *David* comforted himfelfe with it, when hee was in deepe affliction, verf.1. *Out of the deepe I cried.* Deepe affliction, and deepe tribulations, but no tribulation fo deepe, but there is redemption as deepe and more plentifull, *Zach.* 9.11. *By the blood of thy covenant, I have fent forth thy prifoners out of the pit in which was no water*, and hee meanes the *Babylonian* captivity, no comfort in it, but by the plentious redemption purchafed by the blood of Chrift, but therefore wee have comfort.

*Reafon 3.*    *Rea.*3. Taken from our *Baptifme*, which God would have all Chriftians well acquainted with, it was the firft ordinance wee were called unto under the fellowfhip of the Church, and that which wee had neede to live by all our dayes; for the water doth not onely type the blood of Chrift, to wafh away the guilt of finne, nor only the fpirit of grace wafhing away the ftaine of finne, but

water

water in baptifme doth likewife figure to us all thofe afflictions wherewith wee fhall not onely bee fprinkled, as fome are, but fometimes drenched and dowfed all over, as was the old manner of baptizing; this is that wee doe enter into in our firft folemne *Covenant*, that wee openly make with God in the face of the Congregation; our Fathers made a covenant before us, but this was the firft on our part, that wee are dipped into *water*, and yet rife againe out of it, never a whit the worfe, but better. Our Saviour cals *Baptifme, affliction, Mat.* 20.22,23. Can you endure to be fo drenched in the laver of Gods wrath, as I fhall be; they fay they are able, but they fpake they knew not what; but hee anfwered, *you ſhall indeede be baptized*, that is fprinkled, and he feales it, with *a verily, verily*, an *Amen*, that as fure as you have beene baptized into the Family of the Lord Jefus, and your confciences fprinkeled with *the blood of the Lamb*, and the *water* of the Holy Ghoft, fo fure fhall you bee drenched and dipped in *affliction*, when as the Apoftle *Peter* had fpoken of the *deluge of water* in *Noahs* time, when but eight Perfons were faved, 1 Pet. 3.20,21. Hee would figure *Baptifme* thereby, that looke as the fame *water* that drowned the world, yet lifted up the people of God that were in the *Arke*; truely, fo it is in this cafe, *afflictions* anfwer our *Baptifme*, the fame afflictions that over-whelme the whole Earth, they lift up all that are in Gods *Arke*: All thofe that are wrapt up in the Covenant of Gods grace and peace, all

F 2 the

the waters of affliction doe but lift them up higher, farre above the highest mountaines of the Earth. And it shewes us, that wee shall bee lift up out of all these sprinklings and afflictions wherewith God hath drenched us to the skinne, and wee shall finde a bottome and a *deliverance* in due time.

*Reason* 4.   *Rea.* 4. Taken from that which flowes from all this; for God having given us fellowship with Christ in suffering, and wrought redemption for us thereby, and sealed up unto us assurance of preservation in *affliction* and *deliverance* out of them in our *Baptisme*; it is meete that hee that promised this, should bee present with his servants to make all this good to them. This reason is taken from the *presence of God* with us in all our afflictions; so you reade, *Esa.* 43. 2. *When thou passest through the water, I will bee with thee, and in the fire,* &c. which was expresly verified in the *three children* in the *furnace*, *Behold, I see foure, and one of them like the Sonne of God, Dan.*3.24,25. Hee was the fourth that was there present with them. And this is that you reade, *Exod.*3.2. *The bush burning and not consumed*, expressed the estate of the Church of God at that time, which was all of a *light fire*, they were scorched with sore afflictions, but not consumed, *because the Angell of the Covenant,* the Lord Iesus Christ, (*ver.*7.) *was in the bush*: So that hence it is that the servants of God do find some kind of supportance under their afflictions, in their deepest mire.

*Vse* 1.

*Vse* 1. *Ise* 1. It is to prevent the discouragements of Gods servants in time of *affliction*, and to fill our hearts with faith and patience in our worst times, in the greatest evils and sorest *afflictions* that can befall us; in the midst of them all, fill your hearts with Faith and Patience and consolation: No distresse so grievous but may befall the best of Gods servants, and yet no great danger, for there is a rocke in the bottome, upon which wee shall stand, and there will bee safe passage out of it, *Thou that hast shewed me great and sore troubles, thou wilt revive me and lift me up from the depths of the Earth:* His Faith assured him God had led him into the one, and he would also leade him into the other. See how hee stayes his heart by a lively Faith, *Psal*.23.4. *Though I walke in the valley of the shadow of death, I will feare no evill, because the presence of God is there, thy rod doth comfort me*; God puts some staffe of former experience into our hands whereby hee comforts us. This is that which *Paul* expressed of himselfe in his worst houres, 2 *Cor.* 1.9,10. When hee had spoken of his troubles beyond measure, saies hee: *All this is that wee might not trust in the flesh, but in the living God, who hath and doth and will deliver us*: so that afflictions are to draw from us Faith and patience, it is a point Christians are too much ignorant of, when they come into afflictions they thinke no man is so afflicted as they are, and sometimes thereupon call in question, whether they bee

F 3         Christi-

Christians or no; I would only say to such souls, whether were you baptized or no, and if so, was it not into the death of Christ, and were you drowned when you were baptized, were you not rather lifted up; did you not then covenant with God, that whatsoever afflictions you wrastled with and were drenched in; that you would not looke at them as any strange matter; the first day you came into the Church you were baptized, and God made account you should looke for affliction from that day forward, and if they be many and great and sore exercises, the greater and deeper your troubles be, the deeper you drinke of Christs cup, the more sweete will it bee in the bottome; there is something in the bottome will counter-vaile all; you will finde the blood of Christ in the bottome, and the Spirit of grace, and the presence of God there, and if you be dragged to deepe and sore exercises, yet comfort your selves in this, *These are they which come out of great tribulations*, and that will be great grace to you.

Come we now to speake of Gods peoples profiting under afflictions, *They have washed their robes and made them white.*

**Doctrine 2.** *The people of God that have come off well out of great tribulations, have washed their robes, and made them white with the blood of the Lambe.*

It is plaine in the Text; they tryumph with *Palmes in their hands*, which is first, an *ensigne* of *victory*; and also the *Palme-tree*, the more it is pressed downe with weight, the more it growes; now

# The Saints deliverance out of Tribulations.

now thefe that come off glorioufly *out of great tribulations*, fee how they Triumph, and fee how it fares with them, *ver.3,4. The Angels of God fealed them that they might have no hurt*, and they come off alfo with glory and renowne and victory.

*Robes*] you fay, were not many of them poore men, poore creatures, that lived in times of darkneffe, in the daies of Popery, and many of them exercifed with deepe tribulations; poore men, yes, yet they were adorned with *robes*; had it not beene enough to fay, *wafhed their garments*; what muft poore men be fet up with *robes*? Yet *robes* they have, and *white robes*, and *they wafhed in the blood of the Lambe*: So that it fhewes you that the fervants of God that come wel out of tribulations, they get more *royall fpirits* then ever before; for *robes* become royall Perfons and Princes; when *robes* in good earneft are put upon any, they put upon them princely Majefty, a fpirit of glory and royalty is put upon them; hee carries himfelfe no more like a bafe drudge of this world, hee is able to over-wraftle all tribulations and afflictions of this world, and all the temptations, all the profits and pleafures thereof, hee lookes at them as thofe things that are but huskes, fit matter for earthly minded men to feeke for; but for his owne part, hee goes on as becomes a Prince: And thefe endowments of a mans mind they are the apparrell of his foule, when a man hath many royall indowments put upon him, they are princely garments.

But

But why are these called *white robes*? I cannot better expound them then the Lord himselfe doth, *Revel.* 19. 8. it was given to the Spouse of Christ to be *cloathed with white linnen, pure and cleane, which is the righteousnesse of the Saints,* so that these *white robes are the righteousnesse of the Saints,* the endowments of holinesse and righteousnesse which God puts upon them, and upon every Spouse of his, every poore soule that hee hath bin pleased through his grace to deliver out of deepe tribulations.

*Righteousnesse,* both imputed from Christ to us, *All that his perfect obedience and patience and righteousnesse ascribed to us is made ours,* 1 *Cor.* 1.30. And *righteousnesse of sanctification,* not onely Christs righteousnesse imputed, but the Spirit of grace workes inherent righteousnesse in us; *Faith* and *Patience,* and *Humility* and *Zeale,* and whatever grace accompanies *Salvation*; these be the *royall robes* of *Righteousnesse* God cloaths his servants with, when they come out of afflictions.

Why are they said to be *white robes*?

First, what is it to *wash* their *robes*?

This word *washing,* signifies tribulation like water; tribulations are like mire and water mixed together, in which the people of God are afraid they shall sinke downe, and never can recover, untill they beginne to finde there is the blood of Christ in that water, and finding the power of it, their *garments* that were besmeared with afflictions, are so scoured and rubbed off from their own *righteousnesse,* as that they are glad to depend

who-

## The Saints deliverance out of Tribulations.

wholy on the righteousnesse of Christ: neither doth the garments of Christs imputed righteousnesse, stand in need of *washing*, save onely the further assurance and light of it; but the garments of our Sanctification, the best whereof is like *filthy raggs, and menstruous cloathes*, Esa. 64. 6. so bespotted and besmeared with much filthinesse; *Faith* mixed with much *doubting*; *Patience* with much *unquietnesse*; *Humility* with *Pride*; *Zeale* with *coldnesse*; *Love* with much *hollownesse*; yea, our truest *Sincerity* with much *Hypocrisie*: So as that Gods people looking at their owne righteousnesse, are ashamed of their best gifts, and best performances; so that this *washing* is a cleansing out this filthinesse and worldlinesse and unsavourinesse, that is found in our best righteousnesse, the spots that were before found in our graces are now *washed*, and now wee can be patient and faithfull, and our doubtings are gone; whereas love of God and of the world were mixed together before; now love to the world is gone; *Humility* hath gotten victory over *Pride*; every grace is washed by the things wee suffer; and this mire is turned into sope, whereby our corruptions and lusts are *washed* away, but yet there will bee some spots that neede scouring off, and therefore hee saith, *They made them white.* You may have such *washing* and rubbing as gets out the filth and mire, and yet not bee comely, but if together with *washing* they become *white*, that is perfect and cleane *washing*.

G                    Now

Now they are made *white*, what is that? *White* implies three things.

First, *Purity*, they are made *pure* and *cleane*, according to that in *Rev.*19.8. *cleane* and *white* are put together, so purely *washed* and scoured, that now he shines *white*,& bright, cleerly *white*, full of purity and brightnes, so as that now there is some kind of pure semblance and lustre in their (graces) their *garments*, not onely foule spots and greater defilements rubbed out, but likewise the graces of God are splendant and bright and cleare without that mixture and drosse that sometimes lay upon them; Faith is pure and cleane from doubting; Love is fervent and shining; Knowledge and wisedome is cleare and bright; Patience and meekenesse now such as becomes and adornes the Gospell of Christ, so as they adorne us, and wee by them adorne our profession; this is to *wash* and make them *white*; our graces, not such as wee and our Brethren are ashamed to own, but such as both they and we rejoyce in.

Secondly, this brightnesse or whitenesse of garments doth not onely shew you their purity and cleanenesse, but it likewise shewes their glory and their excellency: when Christ was transfigured, his *rayment* was *white* and bright (*Matth.* 17.2.) so as no colour upon earth was like unto it, it did set forth the glory of Christ, and so all such Christians as are thus *washed* and *whitened*, a spirit of glory, and of God resteth upon them, 1 *Pet.*4. 4. so as they now can *glory in tribulations, Rom.*5.2, 3. They are now made more like to the Saints in light,

*The Saints deliverance out of Tribulations.*

light, that rejoyce in the presence of God continually.

Thirdly, *White garments* expresse comelinesse of spirit, joyfullnesse of spirit: When *Salomon* would exhort a godly man, whose works are accepted of God to a cheerefull walking with God, *Ecclef.9.8.* hee saith, *let thy garments be alwaies white,* implying that a Christian spirit, that hath made a good use of his afflictions, hee hath not onely put upon him a royall spirit, but hath washed away all staines out of his old heart, and now his graces are more pure, and more glorious, and more comfortable, his spirit more cleare and cheerefull.

*In the blood of the Lambe* ] that is in the sufferings of Christ Iesus, when wee have made use of the sufferings of Christ to redeeme us out of those afflictions, the very same blood of Christ that pardoneth our sinne in affliction, doth also heale us therein, and doth also trimme up the spirit to an holy purity and glorioufnesse before God and man.

And this is called *the blood of the Lambe.* Christ is called a *Lambe,* because his is *innocent,* 1 *Peter* 1.19. and *patient, Esa.*53.7. because he blood is the blood of an innocent and meeke and patient Christ, whence it comes to passe that such as are drenched and *washed* in his blood, rise out of afflictions, not onely *washed* from *spots* and staines, but are growne to such *Meeknesse* and *Patience*, and to such purity and cheerfulnesse and glory, as they are now made *white in the blood of the Lamb.*

**44** *The Saints deliverance out of Tribulations.*

*Reason*     This comes from hence, it is from the powerfull efficacy of all blessed and sanctified afflictions; and their efficacy is to set all the graces of God a worke, and all the duty of Religion a worke, and by which the blood of Christ is applyed to our soules, and that purifies and glorifies a Christian.

1. See it in particular. First, *Sanctified afflictions* have ever this worke, they first, *humble the soule of a man* before God, *Levit.*26.41. *If your uncircumcised hearts be humbled, hee will then deliver you out of your afflictions;* this is the nature of all sanctified affliction, it workes Humility: And God *gives grace to the humble*, 1 *Pet.*5.5.

2. Secondly, *Afflictions set a worke confession of sin*, *Lev.*26.40. Now what will confession bring? It will likewise bring us grace, 1 *Iohn* 1.9. it will bring us to *cleansing from all unrighteousnesse*, it drives us to examination, and humble confession it besprinkles us with the blood of Christ, and so we are cleansed from all our unrighteousnesse.

3. Thirdly, *They set Faith a worke;* afflictions are called *the tryals of our Faith, Iames* 1.3. 1 *Pet.*1.5. so they put us upon consideration, whence they come, and to what end they come, and *Faith purifies the heart, Acts* 15.9. *Eph.*3.17.

4. Fourthly, *Afflictions quicken the heart of a Christian to prayer*, *Zach.*13.9. *They shall call upon me, and I will heare them:* They learne a man to pray, who was never acquainted with prayer before.

5. Fifthly, *Afflictions set patience a worke*, these tryals

tryals bring foorth patience, *Rom.* 5.3,4. and *patience*, let it but have its *perfect worke*, and it will make you entire, wanting nothing, *Iames* 1.2.

Sixthly, *Afflictions worke obedience*, for they purifie from sinne, and traine us up to bring foorth the peaceable and quiet fruits of Righteousnesse, *Esa.*27.9. *Hebr.* 12.11. So as now wee grow more awefull in our walkings before God; the sinfull failings that were wont to bee found in our obedience are now taken away.

And righteous duties are now performed with much quietnesse and evennesse; before wee had much adoe to pray, but sanctified afflictions helpe this.

It is 1. an Use of *Tryal*, that any of us may make of our owne afflictions; how many of you have beene exercised with great afflictions; some through anguish of conscience; some with deepe and sore sickenesse, some in body, some in spirit, some in estate; wee may most of us say, O Lord, thou hast shewed us great and sore troubles and yet if a man should now come and aske mee, who are these? We may say, *These are they who have come out of great tribulations* within a while, now God forbid; but would you know whether wee are come fairely off from afflictions or no, that wee bee not bemired; that the filth of our sinnes sticke not still about us, that you may carry *Palmes in your hands*, while you live, and carry them to Heaven with you when you dye; Why you shall know it by this: If God have

*Vse*

brought

brought you out of *great tribulations*; well, hee hath taken your old garments from you, and hath put upon you *robes* whatever you were before: If you were to pull a child out of mire, one of your first workes would bee to put other cloathes upon him, God doth so to his servants, and the mire hee turnes into sope, and makes it cleanse us: Whatever frame of spirit you brought into affliction, it will become a *Robe* when you come out of it. Consider therefore what spirit thou hast now, art thou not able to over-looke the world, and all the comforts of it, nor to forbeare the pursute of it for a minute of an houre, why then they are still deceitfull treasures, therefore now gather up a spirit of an higher ranke, thou thoughteft before that the things of this life were great and glorious things; but when the question was, whether you were a live or a dead man; what found you to bee the answer: If you then found the world to bee but unprofitable stuffe, when Gods wrath lyes upon your soule; and have you now a more royall spirit and art able to over-looke all the world, and canst despise thine owne worldlinesse and covetousnesse and all the sinnefull distempers of thy soule, and art able to overcome thy selfe and children and yoake-fellow, or whatever it be, then thou shalt carry a *Palme* for an ensigne of victory in thy hand; but if in this case with the young man you goe away sorrowfull, you will have dirty *robes* put upon you. And further if thou commest faire off, thou wilt finde thy spots taken away,

what

whatever pride or Hypocrisie, unruly affections, wrathfull speeches, it is the nature of affliction, it washes them cleane out, so as they shall bee but little to what they were before; and this blood of Christ will make thee *white*, thou wilt bee adorned with pure and precious graces, with *love* and *Zeale*, &c. and put you into such a frame of grace, as will make your hearts comfortable; sanctified afflictions will make your spirits more cheerefull in a Christian course, and make you bring more glory to God.

*Vse* 2. To exhort you all in the feare of God to see what God requires of you; if God have delivered you out of affliction, you must now walke as becomes Kings and Princes before God, looke at afflictions as they bee, that they are as sope and nitre to wash you, and know that by affliction you have a royall spirit of grace and glory put upon you: Now therefore suffer not a spot to bee found in any part of thy conversation, before God or man, and now walke on with more cheerefullnesse and freedome of heart in holy duties then ever before; and *wash* thy soule in *the blood* of the innocent *Lambe*, and bee patient and meeke for God under any affliction: Let us be like *Lambs*, dumb under them, and not so much as open our mouthes; but if wee bee as proud as ever, as wrathfull and passionate as ever before; now then how poorely are wee come out of great tribulations. Therefore I charge you in the Name of the Lord Jesus, as ever you looke to finde comfort in a day of tribulation,

suffer

suffer not your selves to be bespotted, but a-way with all passions and distempers that before defiled you, and walke so as the name of God, and his Gospell may bee better spoken off by you.

*Vse 3.* It is a ground of comfort to all Gods poore servants, against their greatest *tribulations*, we know not what troubles and afflictions may come, all of us may bee sure to meete with *tribulations* in one kinde or other, long it will not bee till wee see a change, but bee not troubled at it, if they doe come, bee not dismaied at them, what ever may or can befall thee; know it is, but so much sope to cleanse thee, and to make thee *white*, they are but to *wash* thee from thy filthinesse, and to make thy spirit more comfortable, and the frame of thy carriage more glorious before God and man; and therefore feare not the evils that may befall thee in regard of thy Christian course, they will bring thee to such a comfortable frame that Ministers may stand and say, who are these; Some take these *Elders* to bee Ministers, but I take them to be (as in *Chapter* 4.) common Christians, and *Iohn* is the Minister that reveales this to the Church of God: For many times it so fals out that a Minister in a Congregation doth not know the good that afflictions have wrought in and amongst sundry of Gods people: That if a Neighbour should come and aske a Minister, what thinke you of such or such an one, it may be that he cannot tell, they have beene *in great tribulations*; but what good is come of it I know not but

but if they bee come out well, so as that they are made *white*, this is matter of singular comfort, both to Ministers and Neighbours, and every man stands and wonders that afflictions by the mighty power of Gods grace, should meete with such a wonderfull worke as this is, to make such as before were stained and polluted and unsavoury are now made *white* and pure and cleane and glorious and gracious; and this is matter of joy and rejoycing both to Ministers and people, and therefore in this comfort your selves. Onely in this be carefull with holy wisedome in making such a precious use of afflictions, yeeld your selves and brethren and sisters and Ministers, that comfort who shall enquire of you, or bee enquired of concerning you, that you may have come so pure and cleane out of afflictions, that you and they, and all that ever may know and heare of you may for ever rejoyce in this Mercy and Goodnesse of God to you.

*FINIS.*

**H**

# GODS MERCIE MA-NIFEST IN HIS Iustice.

Esay 27. part of the 4. together with the 5. v.
*Who would set the bryers and thornes against me in battell, I would goe through them, I would burne them together.*
*Or let him take hold of my strength, that he may make peace with me, and he shall make peace with mee.*

Hese words are part of an heavenly Song, which the Prophet in the name of the Lord, exhorted the people of God to sing unto the Lord, at what time he delivered them out of the hands of their greatest enemies, and when hee under-tooke to preserve his

Church which hee cals his *vineyard*, *verſ.* 2, 3. and will watch over it night and day leaſt any thing ſhould hurt it, becauſe a *vineyard* of *red wine* (which is the beſt wine, *Prov.* 23.) becauſe even in the Church of God, among the beſt grapes, and the beſt frame of ſpirit, becauſe among them are found many hypocrites, and ſuch as undermine the peace and welfare of the Church. The Lord manifeſts his mercy thus farre to them, that hee threatens their danger, if they continue in ſuch an eſtate, but promiſes grace and mercy, if they turne from it: looke therefore what hee commanded his people in the Law, *Deut.* 20.10. to 13. If they went to make warre with any people, they ſhould firſt offer conditions of peace, before they ſtrike: ſo the Lord himſelfe obſerves the ſame courſe and performes the ſame worke in this place. 1. He doth heere lay ſiege to all the evill members in a vineyard of red-wine, to all the ill members in his Church, *I will burne them together,* a ſore and a greivous threa'ning unto the hardeſt and moſt obſtinate ſpirit, and beſt mounted and fenced with the ſtrength of their owne reſolutions. But as hee threatens what he will doe in caſe they ſtand out againſt him: So hee alſo offers termes of peace, if they thinke not good to try it out in battell with mee, if they thinke it will bee too hot a ſervice for them, let them then take hold of my ſtrength, if hee ſee it bee a ſafer courſe for him; *Let him make peace with me, and he ſhall be at peace*; even then when hee gives them moſt terrible

terrible threatnings, then hee also offers them gracious termes of peace.

In the words themselves obserue the estate of evill men in the Church of God, even in the *vine-yard of red wine*, in Churches of purest grapes, among them there bee such as are evill. And they are called *bryers* and *thornes*, who will set them in *battell against me?* Which though some understand of vices, yet I choose rather with them, that thinke its meant of vicious and evill persons. For God proclaimes warre, not so much against vices as against persons. Therfore this is the estate and frame of evill men in the Church, *they are as briers and thornes.*

Secondly, Obserue heere the danger of such mens estates, when they doe rise up against God, and set themselves against him in battell, will they set themselves, or set one another? who will undertake it, let me see them face to face, what will be their danger? *I will march through them,* (as it is in the Originall) hee will not hinder his worke, notwithstanding all their opposition, he will goe through them, and further his owne worke.

Thirdly, obserue a redresse or remedy to such, in such a dangerous estate, or an offer of mercy to such, who discerning themselves to bee in such a dangerous estate, doe thinke it more safe for them to take a wiser and better course, to come in to GOD, and to yeeld to him, to take hold of Gods strength, and to be at peace with him.

From these words wee may observe three severall notes.

*Doctrine* 1.    *Evill men are as bryers and thornes.*

For of these hee speakes in this *vine-yard of red wine*; as in a *vine-yard*, unlesse much heed bee taken, there will bee *bryers* and *thornes* springing in it: So will there bee in the Church of God, evill men will grow up in the Church, in a Vineyard of red Wine, and God esteemes them as bryers and thornes, the children of *Belial*, *David* then when hee stiles himselfe, *the sweete singer of Israel*, least you should thinke he was in some poore frame of spirit imbittered against such persons, yet it was in his old-age, when his heart was most free, from all distemper and passion, and gives speciall charge concerning good government; and also cals to minde that faithfull and gracious covenant which God hath made with him and his house, notwithstanding his owne and his childrens unworthy walkings, yet 2 *Sam.* 23 6, 7. hee saith, *The sonnes of Beliall shall be all of them as thornes thrust away, because they cannot be taken with hands, but the man that shall touch them must be fenced with yron*, &c. so *Isa.* 9. 18. *Wickednesse burneth as a fire, it shall devoure the bryers and thornes*, &c. The same persons, meaning the wicked themselves. And in *Ezek.* 2. 6. *Though thou beest with bryers and thorns and dwellest among Serpents, yet be not dismaied nor afraid:* So that these are the styles which in Scripture are given to wicked men.

Now for the Reason. Wherein stands the resemblance

resemblance between *bryers* and *thornes* and evill members of the Church.

Firſt, Looke as you ſee *bryers* and *thornes* were the fruites of Gods curſe upon the ground, *Geneſis* 3.17,18. So it is the curſe of God upon ſinnefull man-kinde, ſinnefull Parents, the ground from whence wee are taken, and alſo the curſe of God upon the very Church and Common-wealth and Family, where ever any ſuch live, it is the curſe of God upon them, that they yeeld and bring foorth evill men. *Reaſon 1.*

As you ſee it is in *Bryers* and *thornes* they are of an intricate and perplexing nature, hanging one within another, and ſuch are wicked men who are knit and joyned together in their confederacies, and perplexing practiſes againſt others with whom they live: So the Holy Ghoſt notes it of wicked men, *Pſal.*3.5.to 8. *I will not bee afraid though ten thouſand of people beſet themſelves round about againſt me.* So *Eſay* 8.9 there is an aſſociation, and a confederating themſelves together, implying that there is a certaine kinde of intangling, and a drawing one within another, a folding of themſelves together, to pull them aſunder, you cannot, take men that are inwrapt and intangled within ill company, you may as ſoone pull one thorne or bryer from another, as pull them aſunder one from another; indeed ſometimes, if they lie preſſed under ſome hand of God, they will promiſe to abhorre it and to leave it, but as ſoone as ever they are but unfettered, and let to their owne length againe, that God allowes but life *Reaſon 2.*

and

and liberty, they are againe intangled one within another, *Psal. 2.2. The Kings of the Earth stand up and take counsell together against the Lord and his annoynted*, broken and pull'd asunder they will not bee, especially if there arise any occasion of dealing against Gods people. And as their confederacies are such, so is their conveyance and wrapping up of businesses, closely and strongly and secretly conveied and folded up, he uttereth his mischievous designe, so they wrap it up, *Mica. 7. 3, 4. The best of them is a bryer, the most upright is sharper then a thorny hedge:* So wise is God in all his dispensations, that when hee comes to visit such bryers and thorns, it will bee when their sinnes are perplexed and folded together, the day of their perplexity shall come as if hee would sute them with a judgement fit for their sinnes, as they have folded and wrapt up their plots against the godly, so as by no meanes they can escape them; so they shall bee folded up in a judgement, such as they shall by no meanes rid themselves of, but shall bee intangled within it.

*Reason 3.* As in *Bryers* and *Thornes*, there is indeed an use and fruitfullnesse, but it is but a common use, as to serve for the use of Cattle, and so foorth; for no other imployment: So all the use, and the best service that evill men can doe, is to bee fruitfull and helpfull to beasts, to worldly and sinfull men like themselves.

*Reason 4.* As in *Bryers* and *Thorns*, there is a searching and pricking and stinging nature in them; so as whosoever

soever shall touch them shall bee wounded by them, especially if they bee to deale with the servants of God, as the poore Lilly among the Thornes, *Cant.*2.2,3. The poore people of God living among these bryers and thornes are exposed to continual pricking and fretting and galling; thus they do expresse themselvs; therfore the Lord promises, *Ezek.* 28. 24. that when his Church and people shall bee freed and delivered from their evill Neighbours, then *Tirus* and *Sydon* shall bee no more a pricking *Bryer*, nor a *piercing Thorne* to the house of *Israel*.

As Bryers and Thornes, the best use that is *Reason* 5. commonly made of them, is but to hedge and fence in: So many times it so fals out, that God makes use of these bryers and thornes for the benefit of his servants, so as that they are kept in a marvellous innocent frame to what else they would bee, if they were not well fenced in, but lay open, they would wander and straggle abroad, as Cattle doe out of unfenced pastours; truely so is this case; God doth make such use even of all the evill neighbours of his Church, as that hee doth fence in his Church with them, least they should runne awry, *Hosea* 2 .6. *Therefore behold I will hedge up thy way with thornes, and make a wall that shee shall not finde his paths, they shall be galled if they turne aside to the right hand or to the left,* but God by this means, hedges and fences them in.

Lastly, Besides their perplexity in this life, 6. you reade this likewise to bee the end of them,
I that

that which brings foorth bryers and thornes is neare unto curfing, whofe end is to bee burned, *Hebr.*6.8. they are in the end to bee ftub'd up and dried, and fo made fit fewell for the fire, 2 *Sam.*23.5. they fhall bee burnt together, and fuch is the end of all wicked and ungodly men, without they make their peace, *they fhall be burnt,* as it is here in the Text.

It may ferve to difcover unto evill men that unworthy frame of fpirit that is in them, they are not onely unprofitable in themfelves, but prejudiciall likewife to their neighbours; fee how moft unworthy of all the trees of the Field, they are neither fruitfull nor serviceable for building, as Oakes and Cedars are, but to bee onely bryers and thornes, which of all other fhrubbs are the moft accurfed trees. A man fhould therfore moft of all bleffe himfelfe from fuch a frame, though wee fhould not bee fruitfull in the places where wee live, yet fome good fervice wee may doe, Oakes yeeld fmall fruite, and as little doth the Cedar, but yet they are both harmeleffe and ufefull, but thefe bryers and thornes bring foorth no fruit, if any, it is but for beafts, and they are of no ufe, but to hedge in Gods people, and to pricke and gall them if they runne from God; now what a moft uncomfortable condition is it to bee borne and brought up a childe of Gods curfe: There is a profitable ufe of bryers and thornes, but they were to grow onely in hedge-rowes, this is a fruite of the curfe, that they grow in the midft of fields and paftures, for in all the Paradife

of

of God was nothing that did hurt, but when once the Earth growes accursed, it brings foorth bryers and thornes, in the best soyles, in the midst of Fields and Meddows: So that then this is a cursed condition, there to stand and grow, where a man shall, and is apt to choake the best seedes that is sowne, and hinder them that else would be comming on to Religion, there to live where hee will bee prickes in the eyes of them whom hee converses withall; this is a frame of spirit, however men may please themselves in it, that they can gall and sting poore Christians, but doe you consider that while you soe doe sting and vexe and fret the hearts of your Neighbours, is not this the worke of bryers and thorns, you are a curse to these Churches and Commonwealthes and families where you dwell; this is a fearefull condition that a man should expose himselfe to be a child of the curse.

*When evill men doe set themselves against God, they doe not hinder Gods work, but hasten their owne burning, their owne ruine.*   Doctrine 2.

*Who will set themselves against me in battle:* If they set themselves or one another against mee, shall Gods worke bee hindered? No, I will keepe my pace, so the word signifies, as souldiers, I will pace or march through them, not onely hee will doe that which is good in his owne eyes, notwithstanding all their opposition, but I will march an end, his servants shall not onely carry an end their course, but march, not retire disorderly, nor fly away as men routed and disheartened, as turning backe, giving ground, or yeelding to the opposition brought against them, but *I will goe through them*, that is to say they by standing in the way shall not hinder me, but what I meane to doe, and what my servants are to doe, they shall doe it, they shall goe through with an even pace, and not turne aside to either hand. Gods worke shall not bee hindered; What then? *But I will burne them up together*, that is to say, when their confederacies are most strongly combined, and closeliest compacted, and begins to prevaile with most strength, then God will beginne to set a fire among them, and this will bee the issue of it, when God beginnes to burne and begins to ceaze upon any one mans conscience and burnes that, and fals upon his estate, and weakens that, and casts a fire into a mans tabernacle, and wastes the fruite of his body, and blasts the endeavours and workes of his hands; so hee sets him all a fire, and hee will burne them up together, when the fire is once kindled, it will not cease till it have burned them all up; when a man hardens himselfe against God, and against the good counsell of Gods servants, when God begins with him hee will kindle a fire, that shall not goe out till all bee consumed. There was a conspiracy among the *Sodomites* against *Lot*, *Genesis* 19.9. *Wee will deale worse with thee then with them, and they pressed upon him*, ver. 11. *And the Angels plucking him in, they strucke all them, and it was a*

*cloudy*

*cloudy mist to them, they were all strucke blinde,* and what was the issue of it? Why, *verf.* 24. *The Lord rained fire and brimstone upon them, and destroyed them all,* They rise up against God, against his Angels and servants, and professed they would doe it, then God strikes them; first, with blindnesse, a faire warning, and if that will not serve the turne, hee will burne them up together, foure Cities of them in one day, and God set them foorth as an example of his vengeance to all them that shall come to the like wickednesse: If therefore any shall set themselves against God and his servants, and make battle against him, hee will goe on with his worke in his servants, but them hee will destroy and burne up together; there is no man that lives in an estate of nature, but is in a cursed estate.

*Reason,* My true intent is to speak to this point, how men in a carnall frame of spirit, have intangled themselves in sinne, and thereby warring against God doe thereby draw themselves from the fellowship of Gods grace, I would heerein shew you the counsell of the Holy Ghost; that when Gods protection and blessing is upon his Church, hee would have no man live in his Church but bee better for it; for God saith, *Fury is not in mee,* tell not mee of bryers and thornes, if men will bee such then they shall bee burned together; but yet this hee saith, his intent is to keepe his vine-yard pure and free from these evills, but if they will have peace, let them take hold of my strength, and they shall have peace.

*Reason* 1. Taken from the juſt indignation that God doth conceive againſt all evill men, when they doe harden their hearts againſt him; if a man bee borne in a curſed eſtate, and allow himſelfe therein, and ſo fall ſhort of the grace of God, God takes this as a juſt matter and cauſe of provocation, *Ier.* 7. 19. *Doe they provoke me to anger, and not themſelves to the confuſion of their owne faces. Never did any waxe fierce againſt God and proſper, Iob* 9.4. *Eſa.* 45.9. *Woe to him that ſtrives with his Maker,* God takes it as a matter of great indignation, when men reſolve to live and die in an eſtate of nature.

*Reason* 2. It is taken from the power put upon the Lord Jeſus Chriſt; God hath ſet him up on the *holy hill of Sion, and hee hath given him the Heathens for his poſſeßion, and a rod of yron, whereby hee rules in the midſt of his enemies, Pſalm.* 2. 8, 9. *Pſalm.* 110. 2. Whence it is that there is a wall of fire round about the Church, whereby ſuch as greeve him ſhall bee burnt up together.

*Reason* 3. From the eſtate and condition of Gods people, when God undertakes the protection of his Church, hee deſcribes his Church to bee a burthenſome ſtone, *Zachary* 12. 2. men ſhall cut their hand with it, and *ver.* 3. *Hieruſalem ſhall bee as a torch in a ſheafe, verſe* 6. and like a fire among wood, and all the people that come againſt it ſhall bee as dry ſtubble; and hee will

will make *Hierusalem* as a cup of poyson or astonishment, so as whosoever comes against *Hierusalem*, if hee either refresh himselfe with doing evill to the Church of God, or profit himselfe by it; it shall bee a cup of poyson to him, so as a man cannot hurt the Church, but it will make him to runne madde, which shewes what hot service it is for men to take up any evill against the Church of God, he doth not hinder Gods worke, but hasten his owne ruine.

*Vse* 1. It may serve for a ground of strong consolation to all the servants of God that do bring foorth red wine, well relished, not wilde and unsavoury grapes, carnall fruits of the flesh; if sweete and savoury to God and our brethren, here is a promise of his protection to them, nothing shall hurt them, and if bryers and thornes rise up against them, yet hee will goe through them with his work, and he will burne up all their enemies together: So that when men live in places where they are ready enough to pricke and gall, and scratch at the life and liberty of Gods servants; yet feare not; there are more with us then against us.

I saith a Christian, I should never feare the opposition of the sons of men, but heere is my feare and danger, my owne unworthy base heart is ready to start aside from God, and to dishonour him and the wayes of his truth and grace, and I am apt to walke unworthily, how shall I doe in such a case?

Why heere is thy direction and consolation in such

such a case, God hath promised that hee will march through with his worke, if God give us an heart to submit to his colours, and bring foorth fruites that himselfe relisheth, then this will follow, God will never retire dishonourably to himselfe and his children, however they may be scattered, yet he will march an end, not only in his owne providence, in still mainetaining and keeping his Church for good; but as hee himselfe will looke to his owne, so hee will march an end in his servants, he will breath in them by his Spirit of wisedome and power, that what ever comes upon them, they will keepe Faith and a good conscience, according to all the truth and goodnesse God hath manifested to them, they will march in his strength, and he will keep them that they shall not retire disorderly.

And so it is a Use of Direction to admonish us in the feare of God to take heede (as ever wee desire God should keep us safe from the workers of iniquities) according to the verse before the Text, take heede wee bring not foorth wilde grapes, much lesse bitter grapes, fruites of the world, and of the flesh, and of the pride of our owne hearts; but bee sure wee bring foorth good fruites to God, and not onely good, but in some kinde generous, of the best spirits. *Iudah* is described by the rednesse of his eyes, *Gen.* 49. alluding to that excellent life and spirit that should be in him: the red wine is the most generous, so Christians should not onely bring foorth good fruite, such as hath lawfull warrant from the word

word, and within bounds of calling, but such as hath in it some measure of life and spirit and power of grace breathing foorth in it, and if at any time wee bee straightned, as many times we come off with much flatnesse in duties; wee then complaine off, and bewaile such evils before God, and rest not till God againe renew us and inlarge us, that so God may defend us; or if any prosper against us, wee may either bee preserved secure therein, or if I must and doe retire, then that wee may come off fairely, that God may not bee dishonoured, nor any evill report be raised against the Gospell, by reason of any ill walking of ours; see that there bee life and spirit in your walkings before God in both your particular and generall calling; and then if God transplant us hee will march before us, and wee in his strength shall goe through any intanglements without being insnared, its a world to see the perplexities of some mens consciences, who have ill carried a businesse, and defiled themselves in it, but if the Lord keepe us spotlesse, and our consciences void of offence, that wee walke evenly with him, according to his truth and goodnesse, that whatever exercise God puts us too; yea, if hee remoove our vine-yard, it will not make us barren, but more generous, and fruitefull, wee shall carry our roote with us, and bee set in another place and our fruite will bee more sweet and savoury.

Now for the last part of the Text, it is a direction to all that are not able to make this

K good

good to their souls, that they bring not forth good clusters to refresh both God and man; if wee bee not fallen into malicious opposition, observe we this point,

*Doctrine 3.*    *That such as doe take hold of Gods strength and make peace with him though their condition, were never so bad and mischievous against God and his Church, yet if they take hold of Gods strength, they may make peace with him, they shall have peace.*

Though they bee *bryers* and *thornes*, and bring foorth cursed fruites of cursed ground, that never did good to any but beasts; suppose your case were so, that you never did good in your place, but have grieved all the good ones about you in Church and Family, that every one have fared the worse for you, which is a fearefull condition; but were it so and though perplexed in ill company and cannot get rid of them, yet behold heere God makes a fair offer to you, stand not upon your owne defence against him, but take hold of his strength, and make your peace with him, and you shall bee at peace: Now this is wonderfull mercy; did you ever read of a promise to bryers and thorns, not only weeds, but noysome, stinking weeds, yet if they think good to escape burning, let them take a safer course, and they shall bee accepted.

*Reason.*    Why God so graciously offers himselfe to such and gives them leave to lay hold on him?

1.    First, Taken from the glory of his owne name, when God shall bee pleased to pardon and heale such sinners, it magnifies the glory of the rich grace

grace of God, *Who is a God like unto thee?* *Mica.* 7.18. When ever God shewes mercy to bryers and thornes, such as have pricked and pierced Gods people, no man that sees it, but will have cause to wonder and stand amazed at the riches of Gods mercy to them: Who is a God like unto thee that subduest, that readest downe our high thoughts and imaginations? Who is a God like unto thee that subdueft fuch and healeft fuch fins as thefe bee? This God will doe inftead of *thornes shall grow the Mirtle tree,* Efay 55.13. that this may be for a name never to be forgotten, that hee might gaine a name to religion, and make it famous and glorious; this shall bee to the Lord for a name, to his Church and to such Christians for a name, as are thus transformed from bryers and thornes, a name to the glory of his grace, and the power of his ordinances, it shall stand for an everlasting remembrance never to bee forgotten, it shall stand for a monument of his mighty power of the mighty power of God; this shall stand for a Trophy of glorious victory: And such an enfigne was *Paul,* *Gal.*1.23. when they heard that *Paul,* fometimes a *Perfecutor,* and now preached the Faith, they glorified God in me: When hee was a pricking bryer to the houfe of *Ifrael,* Chrift meetes him in the way, and makes him glad to lay hold on his ftrength, and thereupon hee becomes a tall and eminent and ftraight tree in the garden of God, and the Church glorified God for him.

It is expreffed in the firft words of the Text, taken   *Reafon* 2.

ken from the readinesse of God to lay downe his fury, when men lay aside their sinnes, and God plants a vine-yard of red wine, the Lord will water it, and nothing shall hurt it, and fury is not in mee, neither against his Church, nor the bryers and thornes, if they will lay downe armes against mee: If they will fight it out then I will burn them up, but if they will be saved, let them come and take hold of my strength, and they shall see that fury is not in mee; but let bryers come and make peace with me, and they shall find no backwardnesse in me.

*Use* 1. Serves to give counsell and exhortation to every soule, whose grapes are not yet sweete, that bring foorth fruites to sinne, and are not able to say, God hath filled their hearts with generous liquour of savoury grace: Every Christian duty is without life, if wee bring foorth either bitter or flat fruites, heere is the charge and counsell given to you, to stand out no longer against God, but in the name of God take hold of his strength, that you may make peace with him, but if you still stand out and bring foorth no fruite to God: consider of it if you will stand out against God, and will bee hurtfull and prejudicious in your places, yee shall bee confounded, hee will march forward and consume you roote and branch, but let a man take hold of Gods strength and make peace with him.

But you may say, how may I come to doe it, my fruites are flat and dead, and doe nothing but for fashion sake. I am conscious to my selfe of many evil offices I have done, wherby I have bin an occasion of hindering others in well-doing; but how shall I now do to lay hold on Gods strength.

1. First, If you would lay hold on Gods strength then lay downe all your owne weapons, all weapons of hostility against God, doe not onely lay aside opposition against Gods Church, but whatever sinnefull frame of heart or life thou hast in thy heart or way, cast it from thee, and have no more to doe with it, *Esay* 55.6,7,8. lay aside all wicked imaginations and sinnefull lusts, allow not your selves in any sinne, hee that allowes himselfe in any sinne, hee fights against God: and therefore away with all hostility, and then God will aboundantly bee ready to forgive and pardon thee; if wee would have God to pardon sinne, it is for us to leave sinne; as long as we retain it, God never remits it, but when they shall forsake their evill wayes, then I will heale their rebellions, and my anger is turned from them.

2. Secondly, we are to lay down all confidence in our owne goodnesse, for if so bee that God see wee put trust in our owne strength, in any gift wee have received, wee shall be but weake creatures, and shall still walke doubtfully of our condition: but if wee desire to finde peace sealed up to our hearts, in such a case wee must have no confidence in the flesh, *Phil.* 3.2,3,4. *Wee have no confidence in the flesh, and count all losse that I may lay hold on* Christ; a man must lay downe all confidence in his owne goodnesse and education, and in all ordinances: *Paul* relinquishes all

all as that which had not set his heart through with God, *Ephesians* 6.10.

 Thirdly, To beleeve on the mercy of God, as his great power and strength; if hee shall be good to such as wee are, this is to lay hold on Gods strength, when *Moses* makes intercession for such men, hee would have them to lay hold on Gods strength, and fitly explaines this Phrase in hand, *Numb.* 14. 17. *Let the power of my Lord bee great, the mercy of the Lord is great:* The great power of God is shewed in making good this word of the forgiving the iniquities of his people; so that when a soule takes hold of Gods strength, hee lookes at it as a matter of Gods great power, that hee should ever shew mercy to such an one as he was, that ever hee should forgive such sinnes, and subdue such iniquities, this is to lay hold on Gods strength: Let men come and see and know that God must put foorth mighty power and strength, if ever hee shew mercy to such wretches as wee are: As long as a man lookes at sinne as a small matter, and makes account God hath pardoned as great sinnes as his, and if hee deferre his Repentance, the Lord have mercy will serve his turne, this is not to lay hold on Gods strength, and so long a man makes himselfe uncapable of such a mercy, but when a man sees and knowes hee stands in neede of the great power of God in forgiving and pardoning him, that God shall never forgive such sinnes as his, unlesse *in the multitude of his mercies he put away his iniquities,* as long as a man thinkes that a small matter will
serve

serve the turne, its a signe hee sees not his sinne to bee out of measure sinfull; but when a man sees hee stands in neede of the treasures of grace, treasures of patience, powerfull and great mercy to pardon such great and crying sinnes as his is, then hee takes hold of Gods strength.

Fourthly, Let a man lay hold on Gods strength not onely by Faith, but lay hold of him in prayer and in Gods promises and in all the word of God, and in his attributes and presse God with the greatnesse of his power, and of his promise, and the riches of his grace in pardoning such sinnes as his, and then, saith God in such a case, *let mee alone*, as if *Moses* had layed hands on the power, *Exod.* 32. When the soule holds out with constant longings after God, and will not let him goe till it finde some hope of pardon then it doth lay hold on Gods strength.

It may serve to exhort and stirre up every soule that knowes his heart and life is unprofitable and never brought foorth any sweet or savoury fruites to God to this day, to see now what God calls it too: as ever wee desire to bee free from everlasting burnings (as who is there that can dwell in everlasting burnings, *Esa* 33. last) as ever you desire your soules might finde peace with God, and to enjoy the benefit of the gracious offer, which God now tenders to you; so now lay hold of Gods strength, lay down your quarrels against the ordinances, and all the sinnefull lusts that you have addicted your selves too; as Pride and Hypocrisie, and whatever wee have displeased God
with

with, forsake your imaginations, even your secretest thoughts, and put no confidence in whatever courses you will take, and put not of God, till you come to this or that age, or to this sickenesse, or till you bee marryed, and have provided your children such and such porti ns; and presume of your owne strength and wisedome, this will deceive you; but if you can bring your hearts to this, that if ever God do shew mercy to you, it must not bee a crumme, but a bottomelesse depth of mercy, multitudes of great mercies, *Psal.* 51. Let it appeare that it is power of mercy and rich grace to you that ever you may have your sinnes pardoned, take hold of it, and looke at it as a strong mercy that you must have and lay hold by a strong hand of Faith, and by strong prayers and cryes, and sighes and groanes, and a constant pursute after him in every ordinance of his; seeke God earnestly and constantly, *And so shall you finde him speaking peace* and pardon to you, according to this promise here in the Text.

## FINIS.

# THE WICKEDS CRAFT TO IN-SNARE GODS
People described.

MATTH. 16.1,2,3.
*The Pharises with the Sadduces came and tempting him, desired him that he would shew them a signe from Heaven, &c.*

Fter those Parabolicall speeches which are set downe in in the fore-going Chapter of the *Syrofenitian* woman, the next Parable which followes, wherby our Saviour sets foorth by similitude his Doctrine to the people is this. The *Pharises* and *Sadduces* come to tempt him, and desire a signe

L and

and a signe from Heaven; our Saviour answers them according to their question, hee reprooves both them and their Question, and shewes the ground of it.

It may seeme by the dependance of this Chapter upon the former, that the *Pharisees* and *Sadduces* came to our Saviour to demand a *signe from Heaven,* before hee had fed the people in the end of the former Chapter, where he fed foure thousands of them with seven loaves and a few fishes, a miracle that filled the mouthes of them all with much rumour round about the country, and the *Scribes* and *Pharisees* were not a little exercised therewith, they thereupon to dazell the glory of this great worke of God, come to him, desiring him not to put them off with such earthly signes as he had now done, in multiplying earthly loavs, but to *shew them a signe from Heaven,* that they might see and beleeve; I guesse this to bee the occasion of the discourse, not onely, becauſe this miracle was described immediately before: but becauſe upon occasion of the like miracle, they came to him in like sort, and demanded the like signe, *Iohn* 10.6. to 13. & 30,31.

Now in the words read wee have to obſerve two parts.

1. First, The demand of a signe, *a signe from Heaven.*

2. Secondly, Our Saviours rejection of this demand.

   1. In the demand of a signe, obſerve the efficients or cauſers of it, *Pharisees* and *Sadduces.*

2. The

2. The end for which they did desire it, and that was to tempt him.

Now in our Saviours rejection of this demand you have two things considerable.

First, The reproofe hee gives them, and their persons: *O you hypocrites.*

Secondly, Observe the ground of his reproof of them, and that is a conviction of their readinesse to beleeve more uncertaine things upon lesse credible ground, then they would beleeve him to be the *Messiah* sent of God, upon most certaine and evident grounds, and this he shewes them by instancing in naturall things. *If the evening bee red and bright, yee say to morrow will be faire weather, and it many times so fals out; can yee descerne the face of the skie,* by such probabilities as these bee, and can yee not discerne the estate of the times from all the Prophesies from Heaven, and all that assistance that you see in these works.

A note or two from the words, and first as they may be taken from those that demand these signs, the *Pharisees and Sadduces*.

*Wicked men though enemies one to another, of never so contrary mindes, yea and contrary religions, yet can tell how to combine and agree together to oppose the truth and to undermine it.*     Doctrine 1.

These *Pharisees* and *Sadduces*, they were men of contrary mindes, of contrary Judgements and Religions and Professions, and could not sute by any meanes in ordinary course one with another, for so wee reade of this difference betweene them.

L 2           First.

First, The *Pharisees* they did not onely receive the Law, but did adde to it sundry traditions of their owne, as *Josephus* reports. These *Sadduces* thought it arrogancy in the *Pharisees* to put upon the Church, traditions of their owne, which they renounced, and they did not onely renounce their traditions, but rested only in the five Books of *Moses*: Whence it is observable by the learned, when the *Sadduces* came and tempted Christ about the resurrection, (which they deny, *Matth.*20.22,23.) Christ to convince them of the point of resurrection, he fetches a testimony, not out of the Prophets, because hee thought they would not submit to it, but out of the Books of *Moses*; *God is not the God of the dead, but of the living.*

A second difference the Apostle *Paul* makes mention of, *Acts* 23.8. *The Sadduces say, there is neither Resurrection, nor Angels, nor spirits, but the Pharisees confesse both:* Both what? both the Resurrection of the bodies, and likewise the immortality of spirits; and not of mens spirits onely, but of Angels: And yet notwithstanding wee must not looke at these *Sadduces* as Epicures, though it be the next way to bring in Epicurisme; for if there bee no spirits nor immortality, then they may commit any wickednes; but though they did deny the Resurrection of the body, and the immortality of the soule, yet they did not deny the providence of God as Epicures doe.

Another difference is also noted that the *Pharisees* were more gracious with the people, found greater

greater applause, and greater respect, as being accounted more holy men, *Gal.*1. the strict sect of the Religion of the *Pharisees*: but the *Sadduces* though lesse gracious with the people, yet prevailed more in the Court among great men; for great men love not strictnesse, but rather to take more liberty, and therefore it is that wee shall sometimes finde, the leaven of the *Sadduces* and of *Herod*, or of the *Herodians* put together, *Mat.* 16.6. *Mark* 8.17. They had a conceit there was neither reward nor punishment in another world. Thus they were of such contrary Religions, that they could not stand one with another; but if it come to under-mine the truth and to tempt our Saviour then they both agree together. The same you shall reade practized in *Matth.*22.15,16. *The Pharisees and the Herodians came to tempt him, saying, Is it lawfull to give tribute to Cæsar or not?* These *Herodians* did presse upon the Jewish Common-wealth *Cæsars* governement, and the *Pharisees*, thought it not meet to submit to a forraigne jurisdiction, they did not favour it: yet though these *Herodians* were every way contrary to the *Pharisees*, they agreed both upon this point, *to tempt him*; so *Luke* 23.7. to 12. *Herod* and *Pilate* had beene at enmity a great while; and when *Pilate* saw hee belonged to *Herods* jurisdiction, hee sent him to him, and the same day *Pilate* and *Herod* were made friends; when it comes to the matter of crucifying Christ, then *Herod* and the Jewes and the *Roman* souldiers can conspire together to put disgrace upon Christ.

You have something suteable to both these, *Rev.* 16.13,14. *There were three unclean spirits like froggs came out of the mouth of the Dragon, and the beast and the false Prophet, and they are the spirits of Divels, which goe foorth to the Kings of the earth to gather them to the battell of the great day of God Almighty.* The *Dragon* is the *Turke*, and the *Beast* and *false Prophet* is the *Pope* and his crue: Now though these bee of such contrary Religions, that you would not thinke it possible that they should joyne their forces together; yet so the matter will come to passe that the factors of the one shall consult with the other, and both of them joyne with all the Princes of the world, at least the great Lords of the world, and draw them altogether to the battell of the great day of the Lords, when with one consent they shall fight against, not onely the Iewes that shall rise against the *Dragon* of *Constantinople*; but against those Christians that shall arise against the *Beast of Rome*, and so shall joyne their strength to rise up against the Lord Iesus Christ: so that this is no new matter in the world.

*Reason* 1. Taken from the strong and greatest opposition that is found betweene all truth and false-hood then that which is found betweene any falsehood in the world; there is a farre stronger opposition betweene light and darkenesse, then can bee found betweene one darkenesse and another: There is some blush of blackenesse in all darkenesse; now there is no such disproportion betweene the grounds, and ends and rules

rules of the Pope and Turke, as betweene them both; and our Chriſtian Religion, if once it appeare, as now for ſome yeares it hath done, that the grounds of Popiſh Religion, and the end they ayme at is worldly and carnall, at their owne wealth and uſurpation; and if for that end they make uſe of the word of God, and can make uſe of their traditions to bee of equall vallew with the Scriptures: Grant them that, and it will bee no hard matter to conceive, that when Chriſtians ſhall ſtartle that Beaſt, and the Jewes fall upon the Turke, that when the Pope ſees hee cannot maintaine Head againſt Chriſtian Princes, nor the Turke againſt the Iewes; they will conceive yet, the Biſhop of *Rome* may maintaine his owne ſtrength and authority, and rule over ſuch Princes, by his Canons and Decrees, and ſo will joyne together againſt the Goſpell of Chriſt, and all that profeſſe the truth of his Name.

It is taken from the wiſedome of Satan, who *Reaſon 2.* though hee can tell how to make his owne advantage out of the enemies of contrary factions and errours, one againſt another, yet when they both come to bee oppoſed with the truth of the Goſpell; it will not ſtand with his wiſedome to mainetaine any longer ſuch factions in oppoſition one to another, being oppoſed to Chriſtian Religion: It is true, as long as factions and errours are flaſhing one againſt another, Satan knowes how to advantage himſelfe by their conteſtations and tumults and warrs one with another,

ther, to multiply confusion and disorder, and diffusion of Christian bloud; in this respect the wicked spirit of darkenesse sats himself in his course, and fills the gates of hell and of death: but now in case the Christian truth come to oppose such kinde of errours as are at difference one with another, it will not now stand with Satans wisdome to suffer further continuance of dissention among those of the other side; but hee will then bend the wits of all the subtile creatures hee hath to take paines with the cheefe on both sides, to lay downe their weapons one against another, and to sheath their swords in the sides of a common adversary. No wonder to see sometime *France* or *Spaine* at sharpe warrs: Let them fight, for it hinders not his kingdome, that his owne Subjects should fall out one with another, so it bee any thing whereby God is most dishonoured: but if that Christian Protestants, resist and oppose the Catholike religion, and seeke to roote it out; in such a case you shall not neede to expect a strong opposition of him, and all his instruments; and all the three Nations plotting together, and joyne heart and hand, that with one consent they might fight against the Protestant Princes; and this our Saviour touches upon, *Every Kingdome devided against it selfe cannot stand*, Mat. 12.25,26. and his reason is right; for though sometime one spirit will cast out another; and a good witch (as they call them) will heale what a bad witch doth, or one spirit is too hard for another; yet the truth is our Saviours

## Gods People described.

ours reason stands firme, where there is soe much pride, there cannot but bee much contention, but if Christ come and oppose these spirits, and if hee will cast out Divels, Satan cannot hinder him: If Christ should cast out Divels in the name of *Belzebub*, that's no hinderance to Satans kingdome, but if Christ cast out Divels in his owne name, then its time for Satan to stirre, and therefore now *his kingdome cannot stand:* and so you see the truth of the Point.

> *Obiect.* If this bee true that men of contrary Iudgements, can tell how to sawder themselves together against the truth; how then came it to passe that *Paul* fell upon such a stratagem as he did in *Act.*23.6.to 10. perceiving one part was *Sadduces*, and the other part *Pharisees*, the very same persons in the Text; hee thought that by this breach betweene them in their judgements, he should creepe out of the snare, and therefore in heavenly wisedome, hee takes the advantage of it, *I am a Pharisee,* (saith hee) *and the sonne of a Pharisee, and when the Scribes, that were of the Pharisees part heard him say so, they beginne to contend for Paul against the Sadduces,* and come out with a divine speech, *we finde no fault in this man;* if an Angell or a spirit, that was wont to speake in any of the Prophets have said any thing to this man; let us not fight against him, and then *Paul* was safe enough; now if a Christian

M                                                                  man

man may make such an advantage by that meanes to escape the enmity of them both; how came it to passe, that both these sects did not consent with one consent against *Paul*?

*Answ. Paul* had put the case unto them in such termes, as that hee comes not upon them with any Christian truth, he conceales his opinion of any Christian truth at that time, which was opposite to them both, but onely names that which was onely peculiar to one of these sects; *Paul* doth not say, hee was accused for that hee was a Christian, for such a word would have combined them all together against him; but hee professes he was of one of these sects bred, and therfore they might imagine hee was wholly on their side, and they knew hee was a *Pharisee*, and imagined there was no great difference betweene him now, and what hee was before, and so they shelter him, and the *Sadduces* of the two were the fiercer opposers of Religion: they were sometimes full of indignation, *Act.* 5.17. They raged against *Peter and John*, now therefore *Paul* tooke the best course, hee would escape their hands that were the most cruell, though the other were nought, yet of the two they were the better.

But you say, doth this become a sincere hearted Christian to say, hee is of the profession of the *Pharisees*, which is such as unles a man beleeve and practise better, hee shall never come to Heaven, *Math.* 5.20. when hee
knows

## Gods People described.

knowes they are men that our Saviour had condemned for Hypocrites, and went up and downe to make proselites to themselves: would hee now professe himselfe to bee an Hypocrite, a traditioner, to bee a man that *under pretence of long prayers, devoure widowes houses*, would hee professe himselfe to be of that sect that was ever ready to carpe at our Saviour, would he ranke himselfe among them.

I confesse, it is that which troubles Interpreters, how to excuse *Paul* in this case, to professe himselfe to bee a *Pharisee* in the open Congregation, a great multitude, and before them all, to professe himselfe a *Pharisee*: When as all the world knew, where ever hee came, hee beate downe the whole sect of the *Pharisees* and *Sadduces*, and all their Doctrines and practises.

*Answ.* Had hee spoken in such an audience where he might have encouraged any man weake in judgement, the rather to have cleaved to the sect of the *Pharisees*, that they and their children might become *Pharisees* by his example, it could not then bee excused; but *Paul* knew where hee was; the people that was there, was either such good Christians as well knew his spirit, or such as were desperate enemies against Christ and his grace, the true Christians would take no offence, but would understand his meaning, and for his enemies, he knew he should dash them one against another, and that by that meanes hee should escape, and therefore hee onely instances in such

M 2 parts

parts of *Pharisees*, as in which they did professe the truth; for the resurrection of the dead, and that there is Angels and spirits, and it is true; hee was a *Pharisee* and brought up a *Pharisee*, and thus farre he kept the pharisaicall principles: so that this doth not hinder, but that in ordinary course two contrary factions, may combine against the truth, yet a Christian may sometimes so strike in with one, that hee may seeme not to bee an enemy to both; yea sometimes by an over-ruling providence of God it so fals out, that a Christian may cast such bonds, betweene two contrary Religions, that the Church may fare the better for it, but yet this will not long hold, for in time they will sawder together againe; *Paul*, though hee now scapes by this devise, if hee should have come before them, it would not have served his turne, hee was a *Pharisee* in one point or two, and they thought he had bin so in all; part of the truth, and part hee conceales, and that was his wisdome.

*Vse* 1. To teach all the Professours of the truth of Christ Iesus, neither to trust common enemies, though reconciled, nor to distrust one another to combine in any emulation or enmity one against another, not to trust common adversaries, let them make a league, never so firme as you conceive with us; though they may have just reason to joyne with a Protestant King, and though they now pretend their grounds and rules and ends are the same; yet they will soone breake all bonds and leagues of peace with Christians and sawder them-

## Gods People described.

themselves together againe, and therefore trust not such, and if those that are of contrary Religions, can take a course thus to combine together, to undermine a common enemy, shall not the Church of God so much the more, cleave together with one heart and voyce, with one shoulder, and with all their strength as one man to resist all the enemies of the truth of God, shall Gods owne servants bee so ready to hang of one from another, shouldering out one another and supplanting one another; shall *Pharisees* and *Sadduces* combine together, and shall not the Professours of Christ joyne together as one man, and by one rule and to one end.

It may bee an use unto all men; Christian *Use 2.* men and all men of understanding, not to be led away with the pretences of unity and peace, unles you see and know that you joyn together alwaies in a common good cause; for even Gods owne servants sometimes joyne together under pretence of unity and peace, which is not a sufficient reason; for there may bee unity and peace even against Christ, and against his truth, and against a common cause of God; and therfore consider upon what terms you go, what ends you aime at, this is needefull in all mutuall confederation and association in any businesse whatsoever; and take heede of Satans cunning in stirring up any contentions and strife among the people of God, but keep you your selvs in a bond of union for the truth of Christ, least a common adversary come upon you and undermine the truth of God by your means. Mat.

### Mat. 16. three first verses.

*The Pharisees also with the Sadduces came unto him, &c.*

Ome wee now to the second Point, the end of this Question and Demand; the efficients wee heard, the *Pharisees* and *Sadduces, They came to him and tempted him;* tempting him to what end? Doe you thinke they desire a signe that they may beleeve, hee had immediately before in the latter end of the former Chapter, fed foure thousand men with seven loaves and a few fishes: An evident signe that he that did worke this miracle was sent from Heaven, they therefore did not demand a signe that they might beleeve, but in truth that they might not beleeve; and now, if hee should answer them according to their desire, they would have found a cavill aginst it; and if not, they will set downe and not beleeve, because he will not give them a *signe from Heaven.*

*Doctrine 2.*    *To demand a signe not to confirme our faith, but to harden our selves in our unbeleefe is to tempt the Lord.*

They desire a signe that indeed they might bee excused from beleeving: hee therefore fitly cals them,

them, *verf.* 4. *An evill and an adulterous generation, seekes a signe*; they anſwer that which an adulterous woman will doe, when her huſband ſends a ſervant to her or a letter to diſpoſe thus and thus of ſuch a buſineſſe, and ſhee though ſhee know his hand full well, yet notwithſtanding ſhee will aske of the ſervant a token, whether he comes indeed from his maſter or no, which token ſhee askes not for, as a confirmation of the thing to her, but that ſhee might bee excuſed from doing that which ſhee ſhould doe; juſt ſuch is this adulterous generation; as if hee ſhould ſay, they doe know *that Ieſus is a teacher ſent from God*, and they know that what hee ſpeakes is the word of God, and his meſſage is the truth of God; and that it is his hand and ſeale, ſealed it with the worke of his Spirit, and with the power of his miracles, and yet now they aske a ſigne, is it that they might beleeve? No, but to cavill with the meſſenger, and that they might not beleeve.

But becauſe this point is very ſeldome ſpoken too, this tempting of God, and yet a point of no ſmall conſequence in daily practiſe: let me therefore make it ſomething more plaine, the better to fit it for application.

Firſt, Therefore to ſhew you what it is to tempt God; and then why this kinde of asking a ſigne in this ſort is ſuch a tempting of God.

For the firſt, there is a two-fold tempting of God; one may tempt God as they in the Text, unlawfully, and manifeſt themſelves to be groſſe

1.

Hypocrites

Hypocrites in so doing, they never meant to beleeve.

2. Secondly, There is on the other side, somewhat a lawfull tempting of God. To open them both.

First, For an unlawfull and hypocriticall tempting of God, such as provokes the indignation and wrath of God.

Tempting of God is nothing else but a trying what God can or will doe for the fullfilling of our owne lusts. To try what is in God for that end, to put God to it, to shew foorth his divine hand for the fullfilling of our lusts, to set him a worke to stretch forth his divine hand for the fullfilling our owne desires.

Now for clearing it from the word. To answer you this Question, which may stumble some.

First, How can such a man as I put God to it, to shew foorth his divine hand, and to set him a worke; what can I doe to put him upon it, so as hee should thinke himselfe tempted by it.

Secondly, How should I doe it to fullfill my lusts, an instance of this you have in so many words, *Psal.*78.18. *They tempted God in their heart, by asking meat for their lusts*; in asking meat they put God to it: *Can God prepare a table, or give water in the wildernesse, and when he smote the stony rocke, and gave them water, and gave them bread, yet can hee give us flesh*: Thus they put him to it; doe they aske this to strengthen their faith? No, but to satisfie their lusts, they grew weary of *Manna*. But

But how can I be said thus to tempt God, or to put him to it, to force him or to provoke him to stretch out his mighty hand, bee it his power or any other attribute for the fullfilling of my lusts?

*Answ.* There are three things in the wayes of the sonnes of men, by which God is much stirred up to shew foorth himselfe, and we may tempt God by making use of any of them to fulfill our lusts.

First, God is strongly provoked to worke if wee pray him, thus and thus to put foorth his hand to such or such a worke for our sakes, and hee takes it to bee a stirring up himselfe this way: So in the Text, *They came to him*, and desired him to doe it, as *Joh.* 6.30. *Shew us a signe from Heaven*, there was a desire of such a thing: and God is very sensible of prayer: men doe not thinke there is such force in prayer, as there is, an Hypocrite cannot put God to it in prayer, but hee findes himselfe provoked, not onely out of his compassion to his people, but out of his common goodnesse to the creature, *Psal.* 65.2. The *young Ravens* cry not but God heares them, and *Genes.* 21. if young *Ishmael* cry God heares him; yea and God heares the roaring of the young Lyons; God is sensible of any want, of which the creature desires a supply from his hand, if it bee but the prayer of *Sadduces*, hee thinkes himselfe ingaged by it, and though they do but tempt him, yet it provokes him; though hee shew his just displeasure against their so asking; this sets God a worke and his divine hand a worke, his whole goodnesse is set a worke. But yet there is something else sets God a worke besides prayer.

Therefore secondly, Faith exceedingly sets God a worke, it is an operative grace, whenever it is fastened upon any thing in God, though it bee a mis-guided Faith; if Faith bee stirring, or if it will not stirre, unlesse thus and thus answered: God is strongly provoked to doe something upon any worke of Faith.

Sometimes Faith will force a man to trust upon God for extraordinary blessings, without using ordinary meanes, when they may bee used: this is a delusory Faith, when God offers meanes, if men thrust themselves upon God in that sort: it provokes him exceedingly that a creature dares trust him in this kind, when hee hath not promised to worke: So when the Divell tempted our Saviour, *To cast himselfe downe head long*, when hee might come downe another way, *Matth.* 4. 7. hee answers him, *thou shalt not tempt the Lord thy God:* Though a creature trusts upon God besides and against his promise, it sets him a worke, and were the thing according to his will, it would set him mightily a worke, but however it provokes him much, somtimes a man urges God with a false Faith; such a Faith as in which they will not trust God not in ordinary wayes and meanes, unlesse God will shew his extraordinary power, and that is a foule abuse of faith; men will

will not, nor dare further truft him, not in an ordinary way and meanes, in the ufe of their ordinary callings, unleffe fome expreffion of Gods extraordinary prefence: So in *Exod.* 17.2,7. *Is the Lord amongſt us or no,* they doubted whether the God was amongſt them or no, becaufe they wanted fomething, they would have had fome water by miracle, and becaufe it is not eafily ready, the rockes not powre out water, nor the Earth cleave afunder, and boyle up water from the great deepes; therefore is God with us? though they had plentifull experience God was with them, for hee had by a pillar of fire, led them that way; yet unleffe they have another extraordinary figne, they will not truſt him in ordinary courfe; fo our Saviour told the ruler, *Iohn* 4.41. *Vnleſſe yee ſee ſignes and wonders, yee will not beleeve,* this is not to truſt God in an ordinary way of his providence, but unleſſe God confirme it extraordinarily, wee will not beleeve, and fo God is exceedingly put to it; fo that God takes himfelfe to bee tempted when men will not truſt him in an ordinary way.

Thirdly, Another grace in man that doth fet God exceedingly a worke, and if mif-guided provokes and tempts him much, and that is obedience; for God hath promifed (*Eſay* 1.19,21.) much to obedience, and curfes difobedience, *Deu.* 28. and *Levit.* 26. So that if wee obey Gods will, it provokes him to performe his promife; but now wee may provoke him prepoſterouſly and tempt him, when as wee dare not obey Gods

Commandements, if wee should obey his Commandements, wee feare it should goe ill with us, when in a way of obedience wee feare hard measure from God, and wrath from him; this tempts him, and when in a way of disobedience, wee expect a reward and a blessing from him, a good issue, this tempts God much, *Num.* 14.3. God cals them to the promised Land, and hee sent spies to see the fruits of it: Now when the people heard such an ill report of the Land by ten of the spies, they fell a weeping and a murmuring, *wee and our children shall be made a prey*; so that they durst not goe on to fight, but backe againe to *Ægypt* they would goe, no going an end with safety, backe again is best; but in a way of obedience, they feare evill from the hand of God: See how God is troubled at it; they have tempted mee now these ten times, whereupon he tels them; *Surely this people shall not see that good Land*; because they looked for mischeife in a good way, they should finde evill in a way of disobedience to his will; and so hee takes that for a temptation; then the people discerning their errour, *verse* 40, 41. They tell him they will go now and fight against the *Canaanites*; then saith *Moses, why doe you thus againe tempt the Lord*; But now when they looke for the presence of the Lord, hee will not bee with them: So that you see if the creature shall put God to it, by Prayer or Faith, or Obedience, this stirres up God in this kinde, and it is a tempting of the Lord.

Now

Now men may desire it when it is for the satisfying of their lusts.

When therefore wee either pray, or trust, or obey, or disobey God, for any thing therby to fulfill our lusts, this is to tempt God: So it is said of *Annanias* and *Saphira*, *why agree you together to tempt the Spirit of God*; they intend to put Gods patience to it; to see whether God would beare with them in that dissimulation or no, and to see whether God was so present with the Apostles or no, to see if *Peter* could discerne their dissimulation, and they did it for their own covetousnesse sake. Now when they will try the patience of God, and the power of the Spirit of God, for their present covetousnesse sake, this is to tempt God; they make use of Gods patience to shew himselfe in this kinde, to see whether his patience would beare it or no. So you reade in that former place of *Numbers*, when they desire flesh and water, they desired them to satisfie their lusts, and put God to it, to expresse his mighty power for that end, and this is called a tempting of God: *You aske and receive not, because you aske to spend it upon your lusts*, Iam. 4. 3.

But yet further, this will be better understood, if I shall shew you how farre wee may lawfully tempt God with acceptance from him.

Lawfully may wee tempt the Lord, sometimes in our Prayers, sometimes in our Faith, and sometimes in our obedience in all these being rightly ordered.

Sometimes in our very prayers wee may aske a signe and yet not bee said to tempt God; I meane, not in an ill sence, but it is only to set God a worke to give us a signe.

First, If God offer us a signe, then God takes it ill if wee doe not aske it, as was the case of *Ahaz*, *Esay* 7.10.to 14. But because God in these dayes doth not ordinarily offer. signes, therefore,

Secondly, We may pray for a signe when the necessity of our callings require it, extraordinary callings require extraordinary signes, and ordinary an ordinary signe in these dayes, *Act.* 4.29,30. shew foorth signes and wonders for the confirmation of thy truth, 2 *Kings* 2.13,14. *Where is the Lord God of Elijah*, hee would see the Almighty Power of God that rested upon *Elijah:* And as for extraordinary; so a man may desire an ordinary signe to confirme his ordinary calling. Notable is that Speech of *David*, many discouragements hee had, hee was called to a kingdome, but every man opposed him; his calling was an ordinary calling to succeed his Master in a place which hee was well fitted for, but wanted a signe to confirme it to him, *Psalm.* 86.17. *Shew a token unto thy servant for good, that they who hate me may be ashamed when they see it:* How should *David* bee confirmed in this? He knew hee had a calling, but every man thought it otherwise, and therefore now shew a token unto thy

thy servant for good: What an extraordinary one? No no, but such an one as might confirme to him his calling that hee had in hand, and soe, *Psalm.*41.11. *By this I know that thou favourest me, because mine enemies doe not triumph over me.* If God preserve him from his enemies thats a token to him for good; let God protect him and assist him, and guide him and inlarge him with gifts for his place, and that is a token to him for good; and this is a lawfull demand of a token: Just as *Samuel* gave to *Saul*, when hee was called to bee king, a spirit fit for his calling came upon him, 1 *Sam.*10.9. and this *Saul* might have prayed for, hee was a man fearefull of that calling, *ver.*22. hee said, *The worke was too mighty for him*: But if God give another spirit, hee shall thereby know his calling to it.

And there is another signe; for there are two sorts of signes for ones ordinary calling, one more inward, the other more outward, in some outward providence that beares witnesse to that calling, *ver.*4. that shall bee one signe to him: a stranger shall meet thee, and give thee two loavs of bread, which thou shalt receive at his hand, a signe of encouragement, the sonnes of *Beliall* discouraged him, but those whose hearts God had touched followed *Saul*,*v.*26.

Now in such a case as this a man may aske an ordinary signe for the confirmation of an ordinary calling.

Thirdly, A man may aske a signe to confirme him in his calling, when his faith will not uphold

hold him; *Gideon* was doubtfull, but desires to have his faith helped by a signe, *Iudg.* 6. 36. to 40. and God answers him according to the desire of his heart; and when God shall cast us into such occasions that wee shall see neede of a signe, in regard of the weakenesse of our faith, and the necessity of our calling, or else because God offers a signe, then if Faith bee discouraged; it is not to tempt God to desire a signe, but to serve his providence, and to use his ordinances, and to set him a worke for the strengthening of us in our callings.

And as wee may set God a worke in asking a signe, so in Prayer also for the fullfilling of all our just desires, and especially to fullfill his own will in us, to assist us in our worke, and there is no prayer you so make, but you put God mightily to it, if you pray for a blessing according to his will; hee is provoked to shew himselfe, and to manifest all that goodnesse that is in him for you.

2. But secondly, wee tempt God acceptably, if our faith worke in our prayers, *Dan.* 6. 26. *Daniel* was delivered, because hee beleeved on his God; as if the question lay betweene God and the lyons, whether of them should have most force; hee beleeved God, notwithstanding the kings courtiers displeasure, God sent his Angels to stop the Lyons mouths, and so manifested himselfe to be stronger then the *Lyons*.

3. Thirdly, In a way of obedience God loves to be tempted, and cals not men hypocrites for so doing, *Mal.* 3. 10. if they payed *tythes* duely they thought

## Gods People described.

thought they should not have enough for themselves and theirs; but saith God, pay them, and then proove mee upon that point, and see if I will not powre upon you a blessing till there bee no roome to receive it; which shewes that obedience is the onely way to prosper: obey you, what I command, and sanctifie my name in my ordinances, and then see what I will doe; in this case a man may lawfully prove what God will doe; but this is not to fullfill our lusts, but to performe the duties of our callings, to bee made instruments of Gods service in our places; especially if my faith doubt, whether I shall bee inlarged or no, now proove God if he will not shew himselfe for us.

*Reason* of the Point. It is a tempting of God, because this is a satisfying of their owne lusts, and not asked for the fullfilling of any will of God in the duties of our callings, but to harden our selves in our unbeleefe: If God refuse to give them their desire, they might well refuse to beleeve, and if hee did give it them, then they would have matter to cavill at; Gods will is to give no signe, but to beget or increase Faith; that was the first institution of signes, *Exod.*4.8. Strange tounges are to make men beleeve more strongly, 1 *Cor.*14.22. to satisfie lusts is incredulity, 2 *King.*20.8. to 11. *Annanias* hee to satisfie his covetousnesse; and *Herod* to satisfie his curiosity,*Luk.*23.8.to harden their hearts in unbeleif,to strengthen them in their sins; this is an evill tempting of God.

O         First,

*Vſe* 1.  First, It serves to reproove the Popiſh demands of ſignes from our Divines, they mightily preſſe upon us for ſignes and miracles, they would have us to confirme our Doctrine and Faith by miracles: Now I would know but thus much of them; whether if wee ſhould ſhew them ſignes, would they beleeve, or doe they not aske a ſigne to excuſe themſelves from beleeving, and that is to ſatisfie their luſts, and all ſuch demands, are but ſo many temptings of God: It was verified in our Saviours hearers: Though hee had done ſo many miracles among them, *yet they beleeved not on him*, Ioh 12.37. nor did they meane to beleeve on him: No though one ſhould have come from the dead; though wee could raiſe up men from the dead to tell them the truth of the Religion wee profeſſe, they would not beleeve it. It is ſaid of many of the Jewes, they beleeved *Iohn* though hee wrote no miracle, *Iohn* 10.41, 42. and why cannot they beleeve us, though we worke none, and the ſame exception they make againſt us, was made againſt *Iohn* by the *Scribes*. If wee ſpeake of our ordinary calling, they aske us where is our ſucceſſion from the Primitive times; if extraordinary; then where are your miracles; ſo they queſtioned *Iohn*; if his calling was ordinary, where was his commiſſion; if extraordinary, where were his miracles: Why, he healed many a blind ſoule, and raiſed up many a ſoule from death to life, and fed many an hungry poore ſoul, and were not all theſe great miracles; and ſo if God helpe Proteſtant Miniſters to goe forth foorth in the power of Chriſt to heale ſicke ſouls, and to give light and life to dead ſpirits, and to give them ſtrength and power to walke in the wayes of Gods Commandements. Is not heere bundels of miracles ſometimes compact together in one poore Proteſtant Miniſter.

   This will ſerve to ſhew you a difference be- *Vſe 2.* tweene a cavilling Hypocrite, and an humble Chriſtian: A cavilling Hypocrite alwaies wants meanes to beleeve and obey: Theſe heere in the Text had ſeene even now five thouſand fedde with a few loaves and a few fiſhes, and why did they not then beleeve, why they wanted a ſigne from Heaven; they pretend that before, but they beleeved not; becauſe they want a ſigne, want meanes to beleeve, and therefore hee cals them hypocrites, it is a true ſpirit of an hypocrite, hee beleeves not nor obeyes, becauſe hee conceives ſome reaſon to the contrary, but an humble Chriſtian is of a quite contrary frame of ſpirit; hee ever ſees hee hath meanes, cauſe enough, ground enough to beleeve and obey, he hath juſt reaſon to doe all that God cals for: But oh! The hardneſſe of the heart of an hypocrite: If this bee a ſigne of an hypocrite for a man to cavill at want of meanes to cauſe him to beleeve and obey, then it is a good ſigne of ſincerity to confeſſe before God and our brethren that hee hath great cauſe to beleeve all the truthes of God, and all the counſell of God, but hee hath an unbeleeving heart, a ſtreight ſpirit, and that grieves him to the heart; hee blames not God but himſelfe

selfe for his unbeleefe; so shall you observe it, many men who are not yet in an estate of grace, who yet live under meanes of grace, aske him why hee doth not beleeve and obey: hee will conceive and say, the fault is sometimes in God, and sometimes in the Minister, if the Minister would preach so or so, and sometimes if the Sermon were more plaine, and sometimes if more learned, and sometimes a little shorter, hee would beleeve and obey, something is ever wanting in the meanes, that God provides for us, and there is not enough in it to bring us to beleeve, but if thy heart were honest and sincere thou wouldst not finde fault with God, but thus an hypocrite puts God to shew foorth some extraordinary change in making people such as hee seldome makes any, thou wilt live no where but shalt find Christians many wayes failing, but God must worke miracles else you will not beleeve: If all Christians were so humble, and meeke and faithfull, and helpefull one to another, and so rejoycing one in another, then you could beleeve; but if you goe from *Barwicke* to *Dover*, and from one end of the earth to another, and if you should stay till you saw all Christians thus tempered, you should scarce ever beleeve, there may bee cause enough in us Ministers to hinder you; but its doubtfull, had you other Ministers the Word would finde as little acceptance, and therefore, lay not the fault where it is not, I meane not so much fault, as to hinder

der you from beleeving and obeying, but let the fault bee where it will, there is no fault in God; let us all say, this meanes that wee have is sufficient, because it serves other men to turne to God by; and why not you, other men can bee willing to beleeve and obey, and though there bee many failings in Ministers and Christians, yet they can see cause why they should beleeve and obey, and therefore let not the fault lie upon God, but learne with feare and trembling to submit to the will and truth of God in whatever he cals for.

 Let it bee an use of disswasion to us from tempting of God, and of exhortation, to perswade us to lay downe all tempting of him in any sinnefull and hypocriticall way; lay aside these Saducean and Pharisaicall deceits, meddle not with them, you see how much it provokes God, hee was wrath, because they had tempted him, *Psal.*78.18,22. *and he swore they should never enter into his rest, Psal.*95.9,11. and therefore take heede how you tempt God, you say you doe not; let mee say to you, if any of you shall walke in a way of disobedience, and in a carnall estate, and blesse your selves therein, and still deferre thy repentance to thy last end, thou now puts God to it, to shew foorth an extraordinary patience day after day, and yeere after yeere, how long must God stay, must hee still reach foorth patience, such as no man would extend towards any, take heed it bee not to your owne confusion in the end: *Annanias* and *Saphira* *Vse 3.*

*phira* tried Gods patience till they were both suddenly strucke dead: So there are many that live idly, and take no course to provide for themselvs or theirs, but thinke God and friends will maintaine them; such trust God beyond ordinary meanes, and tempt him to shew foorth an extraordinary power. And other men there are that make account they are grown ripe, and therfore will not pray nor heare; but when the Spirit mooves them, and will not alwaies attend upon the Word; its for them to attend the Spirit, and not to depend upon the letter, and so despise the meanes, it is a wretched tempting of God, to thinke God should reach out his Spirit to build up men in good waies, and yet men use no means to that end, in hearing or prayer or conference; and if we stand delaying and deferring with God till his Spirit bee so provoked, that hee will never offer grace more; it will bee woe to us.

*Vse* 4. It serves to teach (notwithstanding) Gods own people; since there is a kind of tempting of God, which is holy and acceptable, wisely to ponder the difference of tempting of God, that wee may make use of him when wee are called to it; and therefore it is to teach us in some cases, with modesty and reverence and humility to bee so bold as to aske a signe, and yet not to feare wee shall be rejected as Hypocrites for so doing: If God call us to an ordinary calling, which himselfe hath appointed us, and wee finde our hearts fearefull of the issue of it; in such a case you may faithfully
depend

depend on God, you may pray for signes upon that, as *Elisha* in his extraordinary calling, desires his Masters spirit: So many a Minister, God hath furnisht him with gifts, and the people call him out, but he it may be through modesty is timerous and fearefull to goe on in the worke, why now say, Lord heere is *Elijahs* profession, a Ministers calling; but where is the Lord God of *Elijah*, that should now furnish me with a spirit of wisedome and knowledge and zeale, to fit me for this businesse; so a Magistrate, if God put the mantle of a Magistrate upon any of you; if you come with feare and trembling and distrust your owne sufficiency, and aske for the Lord God of that calling, you may expect that God will give you another heart, you may say, *Shew some token for good unto thy servant*, that I may bee kept and preserved in my calling, and enlarged and walke in obedience therein; wee shall not now tempt him sinnefully; but in such a case God takes himselfe wrought upon, and then hee will shew forth his divine hand, In all things we have occasion to use him in; sometimes men feare the losse of wealth and honour and credit; if they should walk in a way of close obedience with God, and so it hinders them from many a good work: but hearken to Gods Word; doe but proove God, and see if hee will not open the windowes of Heaven to you in such a case: doe but proove God; if you finde your hearts too weake, intreate God to strengthen you, and waite upon him for the accomplishment of such promises as wherein hee

hath

hath promised helpe and assistance, and he would then take it for a dishonour to his name if hee should not answer you above all that you can aske or thinke for.

*Vse* 5. If God take it well when wee thus tempt him, and ill, if wee tempt him in any preposterous manner; let this then teach us to take in good part if God should tempt us. God is willing to bee set a worke at our tempting of him in a good manner. Why should not wee doe the same, if it please God to tempt and try us, *Gen.*22.1,2. God tempted *Abraham*, and so God tempts his people, and leaves the *Canaanites* to tempt and to proove them, *Deut.*13.3 *Ier.*3.4.

There is a double temptation God is wont to put upon all his servants.

First, Make account there is no grace God hath given you, bee it never so eminent, but God will take some time to proove you in it, and how you may imploy it to the utmost good; God that gives talents will not have them put under a bushell, hee will one time or other put you to expresse the utmost strength of your strongest grace, whether it be obedience, or faith, or patience, or meeknesse, or love, or zeale; somtimes, indeed through the pride of a mans heart, and sometimes by reason of the unthankfull world, the best gifts in a man are smoothered, and so they reape not the comfort of them. But otherwise, if God give *Ioseph* in his fathers house a spirit of wisedome and governement, hee will take a time to call him to *Pharaohs* Court, *Psa.*105.14. *Iunius* takes it it for the word of eternall life, till the word was fullfilled the Lord Jesus Christ tryed *Ioseph* with many exercises; but *Ioseph* had many excellent gifts, and had hee alwaies lived in his Fathers house, hee had beene obscured: So if God give you gifts, hee will put you to tryall; it is a signe God accepts his people, if hee take pleasure to try their gifts.

2. Sometimes againe, as God will try them in their best gifts, and honour himselfe by them; so God sometimes tryes the best of his peoples graces, that they may see their owne weakenesses, wherein they are most strong; God will have a time to glorifie himselfe, in shewing them their weakenesse, in their best condition. If Gods people faile, it is in their best gifts, especially if tryed by small occasions; if wee be tryed in great occasions, God will in an especiall manner assist us; but in a small triall, in our greatest gifts, commonly wee faile most; *Abraham* a man of an admirable Faith, if put to tryall in sacrificing his sonne, hee can loose his sonne and the promises of life, and Christ in them, then he can hazard the losse of them all: God then ment to try him in his great Faith, and hee overcame; God tryes him againe in the same Faith, in a farre lesse matter, in the King of *Ægypts* court; though God had promised to keepe him, where ever hee came; yet there was hee afraid: See how the faith of this Father of the faithfull warpes in a small temptation, in his great Faith hee shewes great weakenesse. *Moses* the mee-

kest man on the Earth, yet impatience and want of meekenesse kept him out of *Canaan*: So *Peter*, most zealous for Christ; and yet if hee meete with the temptation but of a silly Damsell, about the forwardnesse of his Profession, hee then denies that ever hee knew Christ, and so in his greatest gifts, hee shewes his greatest weakenesse. *Iob*, whose patience was admirable, yet was chiefly wanting in patience upon tryall: *Hezekiah* God left him to trie him, in the businesse of the *Babylonian* Embassadours, and there hee was lifted up, 2 *Cron*. 32. 31. When our tryals are great, then wee gather up our loynes to God, and thinke wee have much cause to draw neare to God, and to pray and to use all our faith and obedience, and then God mightily helpes us; but in our best gifts, if God put us upon weake tryals and occasions, wee commonly there faile. *David* a man after Gods own heart, after Gods will, who followed Gods will in his whole course, rested and relyed on Gods will; and yet even *David*, in a small tryall, when a small temptation is set before him, hee can lust after another mans wife, and soe failes in that grace wherein hee was most excellent. Now therefore looke to it, since God honours himselfe by your trying of him: So if God put you to any tryall, call you out to use all the gifts and graces you have: Bee willing to serve Gods Providence in such a case, and keepe your hearts humble, that God may use you to his advantage, and take heede that you

doe

doe not then warpe moſt when you have leaſt
occaſion, but waite daily upon Chriſt, that
hee may ſupport you, that himſelfe may
receive honour by and from you:
When it pleaſes him to call you
to tryall, and his truth and
cauſe may gaine advan-
tage by you.
\*\*
\*

### Matth. 16. 1,2,3.

*And he said unto them, when it is evening, yee say it will be fair weather, for the skie is red.*

Doctrine 3.

Ee now come to speake of the third Point from these words, and the Doctrine is this.

*That to pretend more ignorance, or uncertainty in discerning the signes of the times, then the signes of the weather, is meere Hypocrisie.*

*You Hypoccrites you can discerne the face of the skie;* you can tell, at least have a neare gesse by the colour of the sky in the evening, what weather the next morning will be, and by the morning what weather the day will be, but can you not *discerne the signes of the times:* a signe therefore that they are no better then Hypocrites, who are better acquainted and able to discerne the signes of the weather then the signes of the times of their visitation.

Now give me leave, first to open you, what Christ meanes by *the signes of the times.*

2 What are those signes of the times, which declare men to be hypocrites for not discerning.

3. Why it is such a worke of hypocrisie.

4. The uses of what is delivered.

For the first, for *the signes of the times*, that (in

a word) is the evident marke or signe of the times and seasons, the day of their visitation by the Lord Jesus Christ, who now came to visit and redeeme his people, according to *Simeons* song; now is the time of their visitation by Christ, from whom they desired a signe from Heaven that they might know this was he. The same is mentioned, *Luk* 19.41.*&c.* our Saviour wept over *Hierusalem*, and said, *Oh that thou hadst knowne the day of thy visitation, but now they are hid from thine eyes:* because they did not know the time of their visitation, therefore their case was miserable, that was the time of their peace, the time wherein God offered them termes of reconciliation and attonement with God, that's the first time, the time of their peace.

Now what were those *signes of the times*, for want of discerning of which, and yet being able to discerne the signes of the weather, our Saviour argues them of meere hypocrisie.

There are three or foure signes of these times of their visitation, which had they not bin willingly blind, they could not but have seene.

First, the time limited of their visitation was now accomplished; so as they could not but see it: The times fore-told of old by the Prophets, and that limited time being now come to a period; *Iacob* had told them upon his death-bed, *Genes.* 49.10. *The Scepter shall not depart from Iudah, nor a Law-giver from betweene his feete untill Shiloh come; and unto him shall the gathering of the people bee;* that time was now expired, the *Scepter* was departed from

1.

from *Iudah*, and was in the dominion of *Herod*, and the *Law-giver* was taken away, the *Romane Empire* made lawes, and ruled as it pleased them. *Shiloh* therefore now must needs bee come, for God fore-told, they should not want soveraigne authority among themselves till he came.

Another time, but under the same head of signes of times fore-told and now come to the period is that you reade of in *Dan.* 9. 24, 27. *The seventy weekes were determined unto the city and people of God, to bring in everlasting righteousnesse*; these seventy weekes were now accomplished by their account, and according to the truth, and this was another signe of the time.

2. Secondly, Another signe of the times was certaine Prophesies, of what should accompany the *Messiah* his comming and what himselfe should doe at his comming. It was fore-told that God *would send Elijah, or one in the power and spirit of Elijah before him, and hee should turne the hearts of the Fathers to the children,* &c. *Mal.* 4. 5, 6. and that hee would *send his Messenger before him, Mal.* 3. 1. and that was *Iohn Baptist, Matth.* 11. 10, 14. Now *Iohn* was come already, and they did to him what themselves thought good. It was further prophecied, that in the dayes of the *Messiah, The feet of the lame should skip, and the mouth of the dumbe should be opened and the eares of the deafe should heare,* &c. *Esay* 35. 5, 6. Why you reade, *Matth.* 11. 5. at the same time when they came to him, hee had caused *the blind to see, and the deaf to heare,* &c. and so had accomplished what he

## Gods People described.

hee had fore-prophecied should bee done.

Thirdly, Another signe of their time of visitation by the *Messiah* was, in that it pleased God to assist Christ, as none of all the Prophets ever wrought before, *Iohn* 15.24. Such miracles as never man wrought, a signe therefore, when they come to aske a signe from Heaven, and see such signes in him, as was never wrought before, at least not by any in their owne name and strength; for them now to aske him a signe, was an argument of grosse hypocrisie.

Fourthly, Another signe of the time of their visitation, which if they had not beene willfully blinde, and had had any discerning of the wayes of God, they could not but have seene, and that was that all the children of wisdome justified our Saviour, and followed him, and depended upon his mouth, planted the strength and stay of their salvation, and redemption in him, *Matth.* 11.19. and that was a signe to them, *when judgement should bee turned into righteousnesse*, *Psal.* 94.3,5. the judicious and right ordering of mens wayes, when that appeares to be righteous; the upright shall see the wisdome of God in it; and the common-people themselves say, when they saw Christ raise the widdowes sonne from death to life; *Doubtlesse*, say they, *a great Prophet is come amongst us, and God hath visited his people:* these were evident signes of the times of their visitation, all bare witnesse to the gracious words that came out of his mouth, and gave up themselves to bee taught by him, these were all evident signes and
plain

plaine to be discerned: *Nichodemus* said, *Wee know thou art a teacher sent from God,* Iohn 3.2. for no man could doe these things except God were with him, and it was not onely evident, but certaine and sure, for 2 *Pet.* 1.19. they had a *sure word of prophecie* for it, and they saw certaine and sure accomplishments of what was fore-prophecied. So that it was evident without all exception, and all of them such signes of such matters as nearely concerned them to have respect unto; but the signes of the weather is but conjecturall, and many times failes, and when they doe not faile, they are not such evident signes; but that a plaine or wise man may be ignorant of them, and say, they were both certaine and evident, yet doe not so nearely concerne us, as the knowledge of the signes of our visitation for our everlasting peace.

 Now in the next place to shew you why this is such a signe of Hypocrisie, that men should bee more weather wise, then wise to see the estate of their own soules, and should be better able to discerne these obscure things and uncertain matters, then plain and most necessary things.

*Reason* 1.  It is taken from the comparison of these two truthes together; these truthes of the signes of the weather, are but conjecturall and obscure, and altogether lesse necessary for a man to bee acquainted with: These truthes concerning the times of our visitation, are certaine and evident, and most profitable and necessary to bee knowne: now for a man to be apt to bee skilled in the wea-
           ther,

## Gods People described. 113

ther, in matters more unsafe and obscure, and to pretend more skill therein, then in matters that are more evident and certain, and more necessary, is plain hypocrisie.

For a little to speake to these things.

It is true, many times it fals out when these signes are given in the sky, that a red evening, a bright cleare, is a signe of a faire day the next day; but the reason of this, is neither so evident to every eye, nor alwaies so sure, nor so evident and certaine, but it may faile.

The best reason given, that I meete with in this case is this, the brightnes of the clouds in the evening is a signe, they say, of the rariety or thinnes of the ayre, in which these clouds are, and is thorowly pierced by the beames of the Sunne, and easily shed or driven away, and so the matter of foule weather is remooved: The cleere brightnesse of the cloud in the evening is a signe that the cloud is rare and thinne, and the body of the cloud piersed thorowly, by the beames of the Sunne, whence it is that the matter or cause of foule weather is discipated. And so for a reason of the other; If the morning be red and lowring, you say it is a signe of a stormy day: So also I say, the reason of this is not easie for every man to discerne, but these men resolve upon the conclusion, whether they know the reason or no. But the reasons I meete with in nature are these in this case; they say, there is some rariety in some part of the cloude, but in that it is cloudy, it is a signe there is thicker matter in the cloude then

Q                                    the

the Sunne beames can readily pierce through; and therefore because of the heavinesse of the matter, the Sun beams cannot drive those clouds away, nor are able of a sudden to dissolve and discipate them into winde or raine; but in time they make account winde and raine will follow: but the clouds being lowry and sad, shew an easinesse in the clouds, now to dissolve themselvs and to water the Earth, and in the end will burst foorth into raine and winde that day.

Now first, neither of these reasons is certainly evident, and every man that observes them to bee evident, yet findes them not alwaies certain: And those that are best able to discerne the reason, and the naturall causes are not able to say, that event hath and will alwayes follow; but both these may fall short of an answerable successe; for though evening clouds be red, and so those thinne clouds likely to be wasted; yet who can tell, but that the Sunne may gather up new clouds, from the other side of the Heaven, before it rise to us in the next morning: and if it draw those vapors after it, as many times it doth, wee may then have ill weather. And againe, suppose the morning doe looke red and louring, as many times it doth, and therefore by reason the Sunne cannot pierce the clouds wholly through, it is likely to breake foorth into winde or raine before noone or one of clocke that day; yet it many times fals out that though clouds bee red and louring in the morning, and of such an heavy weight, that the Sun cannot peirce through

so

so soone as it riseth, but yet by that time the Sun is growne high, and the beames fall more directly upon the clouds, and so consequently beate more strongly upon them; it comes to passe that before noone the Sunne hath piersed through, and scattered the clouds, that you have faire weather after a louring morning. This is evident in ordinary experience, so that there is neither such sure, evident, unalterable truth in these things, nor such evident plainnesse, as these *Pharisees* perswaded themselves there was in them.

But suppose these signes of the weather did ever follow, and the reasons were evident; yet notwithstanding, neither the signes of the weather, nor the causes of them are of such necessary consequence, as that a man should busie himselfe with the observation of it, or the study of the reason of it, for all the use of it, is but for what a man should doe that day; and a man that hath businesse, will not bee hindered by the face of the sky, and whatever the evening shewes, yet hee resolves his businesse next morning, and if hee be crossed, it is not greatly materiall with him. But for a man when hee hath the signes of the times set before him; for a man then not to know the day of his visitation, this being a matter that so nearely concernes him, upon which his eternall weale or woe depends, not to know this, a matter so necessary, so easy to be discerned, so dangerous to be neglected; for a man not to doe this, it is a signe his heart is full of guile and hypocrisie, he thinkes he can see and discerne the state of the weather, but how to order his eftate and foule before God, hee hath no underftanding, *O you Hypocrites!* It is the nature of hypocrifie to bee very quick fighted in points of nature, but very dull and heavy in matters of Religion and grace, *Sottifh children*, Ier.4.22. Luk.16.8. *The children of this world are wifer in their generation then the children of the light*; but in things pertaining to God they are blinde and ignorant; the nature of hypocrifie is to be exact and curious in fmall matters, *Matth.23.23.* but in more weighty matters of the Law, about their everlafting eftate, they are therein blind : not to bee able to difcerne fpirituall things when they are manifefted to us in a plain and a cleere figne; this is groffe hypocrifie.

*Reafon 2.* Another reafon for which our Saviour juftly taxes thefe men of hypocrifie is this : When a man pretends want of light in his underftanding and judgement, when as indeed the want is in the fubjection of his will to the thing fet before him ; they pretend want of light in the judgement, they would have the judgement convinced, that this was the *Meſſiah* fent from Heaven. Now fignes are to convince the judgement and underftanding, no man could doe fuch things as hee did, unleffe fent of God; but that was not the Point; our Saviour truly cals them Hypocrites, there was no want of light to give them knowledge or underftanding, they had fignes enough from heaven and from earth ; and therfore there was no want of meanes to fatisfie their judgments; but

but all the hinderance lay in the wilfullnesse of their owne hearts, they were not willing to beleeve.

Another argument of hypocrisie in them was this, that they are more ready to lay the fault of unbeleefe upon God, not giving them sufficient helpes, then upon themselves, who had meanes enough to leave them without excuse; for a man to charge upon God, the cause of unbeleife, to pretend hee could beleeve if hee had a signe, and a signe can onely be given by God, and they say, they beleeve not, because God gives them not sufficient meanes of beleife: this is the frame of the spirit of hypocrisie, to tax God for want of meanes of Faith to beleeve, which if they had they pretend they would make use of, wherein God was not wanting to give them aboundance of meanes, *Iohn* 12.37. though he had wrought so many miracles among them, yet they beleeved not a signe: God was not wanting to convince them of their unbeleife, yet they beleeved not. *Reason 3.*

From hence wee may learne every soule of us, to stir up our selves to a wise discerning the signes of the times of our visitation; As ever wee desire to have any testimony of the truth and sincerity of our owne hearts, as wee desire not to bee upbraided by the Lord Jesus himselfe our Saviour and judged for hypocrites, it behooves us all to be well acquainted with the signes of the times of our visitation, and much more and better, then with al the signs of the face of the sky; you see how much *Vse 1.*

much it did irke and grieve our Saviour, *Luke* 19.41,42. *Hee wept over Hierusalem, because shee knew not the day of her visitation:* As if hee should say; it were a case most lamentable and fit for any that ever wisht poore *Hierusalem* well, to deplore it with bitter teares; it is a most lamentable and miserable case, that persons and places should not discerne the times of their visitation; the estate of men that doe not know such a time, is an estate of hypocrisie, and a fore-runner of certaine calamity. Would a man know a fore-running signe of following misery and calamity by; this is one (and none of the least) that sure that mans or Churches calamity is neare, that knows not the day of his visitation, takes not knowledge of the time that God offers him grace. It is ever a fore-running signe of a mans lamentable and utter ruine, when a mans friends and all that know him, may sit and weepe over him, hee knowes not the time of his happinesse, and now woe and misery is fallen upon him.

Now because this is a point of more then ordinary use, and yet I doe not affect curiosity, yet me thinkes our Saviour would imply something in comparing the signes of the time, and the signes of the weather together. And God having usually made this world to be a mappe and shaddow of the spirituall estate of the soules of men: therefore give me leave for the better discerning of things in this kinde; learne wee to discerne the signes of our owne times; for the signes of the weather in which our Saviour makes his comparison, rifon, and there are certaine fignes and feafons of the weather to which a man may compare the eftate of his owne time and feafon.

There are 3. or 4 feafons and times of vifitation, which it behooves Chriftians to know them well, as they would avoid the imputation of hypocrifie and prevent danger of calamity.

Firft, There be times and fignes of times of grace offered, that is, the times in which God vifits men with offers of grace.

Secondly, There be times and fignes of times of grace received, and it is a very needfull thing to know the time and figne of it.

Thirdly, There be alfo times and figns of times of graces decaying and withering.

Fourthly, there be fignes of times of judgments removed, and of mercies breaking in upon us.

Fifthly, there be alfo times of judgements threatned, and fignes of their breaking in upon us.

All thefe Chriftians fhould be well acquainted with, and if not, you fee it is taxed by our Saviour of palpable hypocrifie.

Firft, (becaufe J would go no further then the Text) See it as in the face of the sky, God hath laied downe a right obfervation of the fignes of our vifitation: How fhall I difcerne the fignes of the times of the vifitation of my owne foule, for grace offered; that this is the time that God offers grace to my heart, that J doe not out-fit my time: How fhall J know it? How doe you difcerne that God cals you to your bufineffe, to walke about the duties of your particular calling: by the
fame

1.

same, may you discerne, when God cals you to accept the offers of grace; the Apostle gives us evident light in this kinde, *Rom.* 12.11,12. *It is high time now for us to awake out of sleepe;* how doth hee know that? why the night is farre spent and the day is at hand; a man knowes his time to rise, hee will for shame get up, when the day breaks and the Sunne arises, and shines in at his window. And is it not high time for a man to awake out of the darknesse of ignorance, and the sleepe of carnall security, when the light of the Gospell shines cleerly, and the Sonne of Righteousnesse arises with healing in his wings, and stares into our minds and consciences, and will not suffer us to sleepe, but will so forceably enter in, that wee cannot but see and heare and bee converted, unlesse wee will be wilfully blinde: when the day dawnes and the day starre arises in our hearts, is it not now time to rise, 2 *Pet.* 1.19. The *Law* was *a light*, but it was in a Lanthorne, or in a *darke place, and was not easily discerned, but in the end the day starre appeares*, that is the preaching and dispensation of the Gospell, and the Sonne of Righteousnesse closely followes the preaching of the Gospell, and so displayes and manifests himselfe, even as the Sunne followes the day starre; it is called the Shepheards starre, the day starre; and so this starre of the Gospell is the Shepheards starre; the Ministers are starres when they arise with cleare and pure dispensations of the Gospell, and manifestations thereof in the faces and hearts of the sonnes of men: Christ him-

himselfe followes close the pure ministration of his Gospell, and that's the day of salvation; the very signe of the time of grace offered, the time when the day starre arises, if a man discerne not that to be his time, and put it off from this time to that, thou knowest not how soone this day starre may be taken away, and the Sunne wrapt up in a cloude; and then mayest thou goe farre enough to seeke the like offers of grace, that heere thou hadst dispenced and never finde them; and therefore it behooves men to take notice of the signes of the times of their visitation: *Arise my Love, my Dove, and come away*, Cant. 2. 10. to 13. whence must shee come? from the Babilonian darkenesse; why so, what is the signe of her time to arise? *For the winter is past and the Spring drawes on; the raine is over, the flowers appeare in the earth; the time of the singing of birds is come, and the voyce of the Turtle is heard in our land*, &c. *Arise my faire one and come away*; See how hee presses her againe and againe and now to arise, and now it is the time of her visitation and offer of grace, when the winter is past, when the coldnesse and darkenesse of ignorance and security and superstition is past; and when the birds begin to sing, and the voyce of the Turtle is heard; a bird famous for mourning after her mate; when the time is come, that God stirres up his Prophets in *Iudah* as *Zacharia, Habbakkuk* and others, when they begin to sing; and good Levites and good Ministers, tuning their notes, and tuning for

R  the

the good of the people, and Christ mourning for want of his Spouse, and for the hardnesse of mens hearts, and longing for the conversion of the people, and wooing and alluring them to come home unto him; when this is heard in the Land, there is the face of a spring: some shew of godly ones, to come on to the wayes of Gods grace, and so some hopefull springing buds arising in the hearts of Gods servants. This is one signe of the time of our visitation, when God beginnes thus to shine upon us by the light of his Gospell, and the beames of his Spirit, and knockes thereby at our hearts, and yet wee love to sleepe and will draw about us the curtaines of carnall security, and of our owne lusts. Now it is high time to awake; O yee Hypocrites, can yee tell when to arise in the morning, and when to goe about your businesse, and to stirre your selves about your labours, and cannot you tell when it is time to awake out of your blinde courses, wherein you have lyen so many yeares together.

2. The second time is the signes of the times of grace received, and that is worthy any mans knowledge, to know the time, when God hath risen to his heart, and had respect to the frame of his spirit, and promising faire weather; when the evening is red, you say it will bee faire weather, for the sky is red; so in this case, if God have beene pleased to vouchsafe to any Christian heart a blushing rednesse, a bright rednesse of countenance, for sence and shame of all his former evill wayes,

## Gods People described.

wayes, it is an evident figne of faire weather arifing to the foule, *Ezra 9.6. O my God I am a-shamed and blush to lift up my face to Heaven:* After that God had done all those great things for them, God had given them a naile in his Tabernacle, and had given them a breathing time, and yet now againe they have returned to evill: now sayes hee, *I am ashamed and blush to lift up mine eyes to Heaven;* so *Ezra 10.2. There is hope of Israel*, there is hope of *Reformation*, when God gives his people hearts to blush for shame for all the evils they have done in his sight, a signe God hath an intendment to doe them good; when a man blushes and shames for sin, it is a signe that he grieves for it as it is, vile and filthy; not as it is dangerous to his soule or breedes honour to his conscience, for that a man more feares, then he is ashamed of: when a man is ashamed of sinne in the presence of God, hee blushes at it, and his heart is confounded in him, for what hee hath done, *Ier. 31.18,19. I am confounded and ashamed, because I did beare the reproach of my youth:* When therefore it pleases God to give a man a blushing shame; for that hee should live so long and understand so little; sees so many examples of Piety and Godlinesse before him, and himselfe so sinnefull, and is inwardly ashamed, and outwardly blushes at this; there is faire weather toward.

Yea further, there is faire weather towards though these red clouds do but appeare in the evening of a mans dayes, if in the evening of a mans life

life, his heart be pierced with shame and blushing for all the vileneffe of his courfe before God, and unworthy dealing with God; that he fhould put God to it, to waite upon him fo long; if there be then thefe red clouds of blufhing, it is a good figne of an happy morning of refurrection in another world: on the other fide, if as you read, *Ier.6.15.* they were not at all afhamed, they could not blufh for all the evils they had done: therefore faith God in the day of their vifitation they fhall fall, and never rife againe; there is a figne of foule weather, when men are convinced of finne, and yet cannot blufh upon fuch occafions as this, then they fhall fall and rife no more.

But as a fecond figne of faire weather, it was you heard, if the cloudes were thinne, and the bright beames of the Sunne had throwly pierced and inflamed them, fo that no longer thickneffe and darkeneffe was remaining, the Sunne would foon difpatch them away; but when the sky is red and lowring, there is a figne of foule weather, becaufe the Cloudes were too maffie, too weighty and heavy to be remooved, and becaufe of that, I am apt to thinke Chrift would give us fome light for interpretation of this word, by a word the Evangelift feemes to apply to this point, in what you read in the like cafe, concerning the young man in the Gofpell, hee comes to Chrift in the morning of his age, *Matth.19.16.* and *Mark.10.17.* Hee expreft fo much, as that the Text faith,

faith, *Chriſt looked upon him and loved him;* there was a bluſh of colour of vertue in him, and had he come on and beene a bright cloud, and had beene throughly pierced, and enflamed with the beames of Chriſts love, hee had had faire weather in this world and in another, but hee could not yeeld to all that was laied downe before him, there was too much thickneſſe in his heart; and the ſame word uſed heere for lowring is there uſed, *Mark.* 10.22. Hee was ſad at that ſaying, in the Originall it is, συγνάσας, and ſo it is ſad and lowring; hee was laden with a deale of thickneſſe, ſuch as would not ſuffer him to yeeld to Chriſt, but hee goes away lowring; when therefore it comes to this, that the beames of the bright light, and Sunne-ſhine of the Goſpell ſhines into the heart, and hee will ſet himſelfe to this duty, and to that, but in the end hee comes to meete with ſomething that is a little to unweildy for him, and then it comes to a συγνάσας, there will be a ſtorme that day; and thereupon ſaith our Saviour, *O how hard is it for a rich man to enter into the kingdome of Heaven:* Soe that you may eaſily ſee what a fearfull ſtorme waites upon ſuch a ſoule that hath a louring reſiſtance againſt the bright beames of the Lord Ieſus Chriſt, nay rather that riſes up againſt that light, hee will in the end bee red and louring, and that louring time of his is a forerunning ſigne, of a deſperate ſtorme that will drench ſuch a ſoule to the skinne, hee shall

shall fall, and be utterly caſt downe; but otherwiſe when the ſoule is in this frame, that there is nothing to doe or ſuffer; but hee is ready to doe and ſuffer it, there is in him a bluſhing for ſhame of ſinne committed, and there is no wraſtling nor ſtrugling againſt the wayes of Gods grace; but whatever light the Lord Ieſus ſends, hee is pierced through with it, and when then all miſts are remooved and ſcattered, faire weather is then a comming on.

3. A third ſigne of the time of our viſitation is in reſpect of the ſignes of the decayes of growth in grace. How may I know that grace is decaying, or that grace is growing, and there is ſignes of both.

Firſt, You know it is a cauſe of darkening the Moone, if there be an interpoſition of the body of the Earth, betweene the Sunne and it, and it is a cauſe of the ecclipſe of the Sun, when the body of the Moone is interpoſed betweene the Sunne and the Earth; ſo it is an evident ſigne of the decay of grace in any, when earthly things begin to take place in the heart of a man, when a man ſets his heart upon earthly things, when they come betweene a mans heart and the Lord Ieſus Chriſt the Sonne of Righteouſneſſe, then there is an ecclipſe of grace, and that will grow more and more, and if there proove an ecclipſe in this caſe, grace will decay. If that *David* fall upon *Bathſheba*, the ſtaffe of his lively grace will be broken,

broken, when any thing takes up the heart, any lust whatsoever it will cloud and over-top the best seed of the word in a man; it will wholly darken the best hypocrites; and it dams up Gods peoples graces exceedingly, as in respect of the cares of this world; if a mans heart be set upon these, as that hee doth not enjoy the things of this life in the Lord and for the Lord, and from the Lord, but looses God in the creature; if a man loose Christ in the honours and pleasures of this world, there is an ecclipse towards, and it is already begun. Whereas on the other side, if a man have and keepe an heart open to heavenly things, that the dewes of Heaven are not restrained, and the light of the Sunne is shining upon him, it is an evident signe of the increase of grace; when doth the Moone increase? is it not when she is gathering towards the Sunne, and the beames of the Sunne doe clearely cast themselves upon the Moon, and the nearer she gathers to the Sunne, she gathers and increaseth more and more in light; and when the Earth lyes most open to the dewes of Heaven, and the bright beames of the Sunne, is not then most fruitefull, *Job* 38.31. These were influences of the seven starrs, that rise in the spring and set in Autumne, and that bring sweet Aprill shores; when the Earth lyes open to the dews of heaven, and to the bright beames of the Sunne, it growes warme and fruitefull, and so becomes both pleasureable and profitable: So when the word

word of God (which the Holy Ghoſt compares to theſe ſweet influences, *Deut.* 32. 2.) when a man comes to the word, and findes that the ſweete influence of the Spirit there is not reſtrained nor ſtraightned; but the word drops like Heavens dew upon his ſoule, and that upon all the parts of his ſoule and body, as being open to receive it; grace is ſpringing now, and the fruits thereof is growing up in his ſoule, and it will thrive more and more, when hee ſees the face of Chriſt in the Goſpell, hee is transformed into the Image of Chriſt, 2 *Cor.* 3. 18. and hee goes on from one glorious grace unto another, when there is nothing lies betweene a mans ſoule and Heaven, its a wonder to ſee the ſtrange growth of it, otherwiſe if the caſe ſtand, as you read, *Levit.* 26. 19. when the Heaven is as yron, the Earth will ſoone be as braſſe, when the heart beginnes to feele no power in Gods holy and pure ordinances, no bedewing of his ſoule, from theſe the heart will ſoone grow barren and unfruitfull, and will bring foorth nothing but bryers and brambles; yea, and this may bee the caſe of Gods owne ſervants.

Another ſigne of grace decaying is this: If a Chriſtian be growne up to ſome ſelfe-fullneſſe, it is a fore-running ſigne of grace decaying, when you once become ſecure and to reſt in the fullneſſe of your owne ſtrength, becauſe the favour of God hath beene full upon you, and grace richly communicated to you; if you now grow bigg and full, then look for a wain ſhortly, when is the

Moon

Moone neareſt to its waine? is it not when ſhee is full in her owne orbe, though ſhee received it all from the brightneſſe of the Sunne: So ſoone as the Sunne is Eaſt and the Moone Weſt, the next quarter ſhee decreaſes, and ſo extinguiſheth, that ſhortly no beames of the Sunne will ſhine upon her: So is it with a Chriſtian; when was the Moone in full with *Peter*, was it not when hee came out with this ſaying, *Though all men deny thee yet will not I*, *Matth.* 26. 33,35. hee was very ſelfefull when hee thinkes hee can ſticke cloſer to Chriſt then all the reſt of his fellow Diſciples, and might you not then have fore-told him, what a woefull waine hee was now falling into, as indeed hee did that night, ſo *Pſalm.*30.6,7. *I ſaid in my proſperity I ſhall never be mooved*, it was full Moone now with *David*; but hee was ſoone in the waine, and preſently ſhattered, and not a ſparke of his heroyicall ſpirit left in him: Indeed, *Pſalm. 3*. *David* was in good plight, when his faith recovered againe, and then hee feared not for ten thouſand that roſe up againſt him; but otherwiſe when he begins to fall, his heart failes him; but when a man is full of the Lord Jeſus, ſtrong in his might and weake in himſelfe, *Prov.* 30. 2,3. When a man beginnes to finde himſelfe to bee nothing, and yet can doe more ſervice for God then his fellowes, 1 *Cor.*15.10. and knowes how to doe any thing through Chriſt that ſtrengthens him, *Phil.*4.11,12,13. that man is growing and thriving; and the more a man feeles his want of

S          Chriſt

Chrift, the more hee cleaves to him, and the more he hath, the more hee would have of him, to ftand faft in that liberty wherein Chrift hath fet him, now God *gives grace to the humble*, 1 Pet. 5. 5.

3. Thirdly, It is a figne of grace decaying, when a man growes heavy and drowfie and undifpofed to good duties. When was it that the Difciples began to faile? was it not when Chrift comes again and againe and findes them drowfie and heavy, *Matth.* 25. 41, 42. when they could neither watch nor pray, and then the iffue of it was, *they forfooke him.* Is it not a figne of finne growing upon a man, When hee cannot hold open his eyes in a good duty? when a man growes drowfie in prayer and hearing, fome temptation is now a growing faft upon him; but if a man grow more lively, and fpirituall and vigilant, that man is in a faire way to ftand faft in all temptations.

4. Now for the 4th and laft, and that is fignes of the times of Judgement, both approaching and remooving, or of judgements remooving, or mercies approaching, and there are figns of both; both thefe times doe paffe over us, and how fhall wee difcerne them? For this I cannot give you a better figne from the face of the sky then God himfelfe gives in *Genefis, If you finde and perceive a bright raine-bow in a watery cloud, it is an evident figne the ftorme is a breaking up, and will be gone and blow over,* Gen. 9. 13, 17. The Lord hath fworn he will no more over-flow the whole earth with waters, and therfore for a figne of the
Cove-

## Gods People described.

Covenant, hee hath set his bow in the cloud, and if it appeare the storme will shortly over. Now what is that? to apply it to the signes of the times of our visitation, when wee may know that a judgement is ready to remoove. What is Gods bow? In Scripture phrase, the bowe of a man, is the bent of a man. As *Joseph* his Bowe abode in strength, *Gen.* 49. 24. The bent of his spirit still stood at the full bent and strength in the midst of all discouragements, and did not slug it, though his Brethren, and his Mistris, and his Master, and every one shot sore at him, yet his bow abode in strength; it was old *Jacobs* blessing to him, and so the bent of his spirit abode in strength and in vigour, hee still held his integrity; then Gods bow is Gods bent; a signe that the storme is a blowing over, and faire weather is towards, what is the matter, if God but set a firme resolution, a spirituall gratious disposition, an inclining and bowing of the soule that hee bend the hearts of men to God, and to the waies of his grace, and that in a watery cloude, that is, in a soft and melting heart, then there is no judgement will lye long upon that soule, and no mercy will be long with-held from him; if the heart be strongly bent to walke with God, and that not in the pride of a mans spirit; but in a melting frame of spirit, such an one as this, whatever storms were upon him, now all judgements are a blowing over, and faire weather is towards, and such as that a man may know, there will be the brightnesse of Gods face upon his soule and his favour to refresh his heart in all inward and outward occasions. *David* when he was full of his owne strength, suddenly in a cowardly manner (if I may so speake) his heart grew dead within him, yet before hee was got to *Mahanaim*, hee gathered up his spirits again, and girds up his vigour and strength afresh, and then hee got a firme bent of a Christian spirit; this is Gods bow in the soule of a Christian man; but what cloude was it in? Had it beene a stiffe resolution of his owne strength, it had failed him, but it was in a watery cloude, hee and his people went up to Mount *Olivet*, weeping, 2. *Sam.* 15.26. to 30. and was growne into such a melting frame, as that when the Priests would have carried the Arke after him, nay, saith hee, *Carry it backe againe: If the Lord say I have pleasure in David, he will bring me backe againe, but if not, here am I, let the Lord doe with me what seemeth him good:* Heere is now a melting watery cloude, the beams of the Sonne of righteousnesse had pierced it through, which fore-tels the ruine and destruction of all danger, and shewes that *Davids* restoring is neare. As the heart grows more humble and melting before God, and more firme and resolute in the Lords strength, so doth any calamity disperse it selfe, and any mercy breake in upon us: There are many excellent promises in *Job* 5.17. to the end of the Chapter, made to that soule, that is well taught and nurtured by affliction, and there are many other promises made to peace and acquaintance with God, *Iob* 22.

from

from *verf.* 21. to the end of the Chapter; now in such a case as this, when this is the bent of a Christian; when a man is so nurtured by affliction, as that hee growes more patient, and more humble and loving, and that a man thereupon acquaints himselfe with God, and puts away all iniquity out of his heart and hands, and if God then help us to live humbly and meltingly under his hand, and we blesse him for his providence, it is such an evident fore-runner of evill avoiding and good a comming, as indeed nothing is more; and this wee must bee sensible of, as ever we desire to have any signes of comfortable dayes approaching, to grow strong in our bent in the waies of grace, and in that meekenesse and lowlinesse, and melting frame of heart, as that you may see Gods raine-bow is set in a watery cloude, looke now for all stormes to blow over, but if you see that the bent of a mans spirit begin to slug it, it is an evident signe of a storme approaching: a weather gall, is but a peece of a rain-bow, and hangs not from one end of the sky to another; and so it is a fore-running signe of foule weather, which holds foorth thus much, when men will doe no more then they thinke good of, deale by peece-meale with God: a storm is a comming to deal otherwise with them, if they belong to God; when the Church of *Ephesus* had un-bent her spirit, and lost her first love, would not now keepe so close to God, nor manifest her selfe so much for God in a way of God, as sometimes she had done, it was a signe that darkenesse and trouble,

S 3      and

and danger was a comming to that Church, *Rev.* 2.3,4. And which is yet a worse signe, when a man is bent against God, and the wayes of his grace, and the Divels bow is set in a man, I know that then the Lord is determined to bring mischiefe upon such a man, 2 *Chron.*25.16. *I knew the Lord is determined to destroy thee*, how did hee know that? Hee saw the Divels bow bent in the heart of the King, when hee saith to the *Prophet, Hold your peace who made you of the Kings counsell:* So that if you see the Divels bent in a man, that hee sets himselfe against God, and the wayes of his grace, hee will be left to most woefull mischiefe, according to that in 1 *Sam.*2.24,25. *They hearkened not to the voyce of their father, because the Lord would destroy them:* They would not bee ungirt from their wicked course they had beene addicted too, and that's a manifest signe that God will destroy them.

*Vse 2.* This serves to shew you, that it is not utterly unlawfull for men to make observation of the estate of the weather, and face of the sky; our Saviour doth not reproove it in them, but onely reprooves this, in that they were better skilled in the face of the sky, and signes of the weather, then in the signes of the times, *Luk.* 12.54,55. *When yee see a cloude rise out of the West, straightway yee say there comes a shore, and so it is, and when yee see the South winde blow, yee say there will be hease, and it commeth to passe,* &c. hee rejects not such kind of conjectures, there is a workemanship of God in them, nor doth hee mislike the study of nature. Let

## Gods People described.

*Vse 3.* Let what you have heard be a provocation to every soule of us to take heed and beware of hypocrisie, you see how loathsome it is to Christ, hee never speakes worse word then this, *O yee hypocrites*, when hee speakes with most detestation, yet this is the worst word hee speakes of any men, *O yee hypocrites*, and therefore farre be it from the spirits of Christian men, Abhorre you all seeds of hypocrisie, its very loathsome to God, when he threatens the worst evill to the worst sort of Ministers that ever the Church of God bore, *Matth.*24.51. What will the Lord of such a Steward doe, when hee comes to give him his portion with hypocrites and unbeleevers, a man would be loath to be coupled with a drunken quarrelsome Roister, A man would blesse himselfe from fellowship with such a man while hee lives, yet if a man be an hypocrite, hee shall be ranked with such companions in hell; if therefore thou wouldest have no fellowship with such spirits and unfruitefull workes of darkenesse, blesse thy selfe from hypocrisie, *God loves truth in the inward parts, Psal.*51.6. better lye open to lesse torment, then to be yoaked with such deboyst spirits in another world.

## FINIS.